ALIENATION DISPLACEMENT
AND
REHABILITATION

ALIENATION DISPLACEMENT
AND
REHABILITATION

S. Bosu Mullick
Samyadip Chatterji
Subaltern Consultants Trust

Under the auspices of
William Carey Study and Research Centre

Uppal Publishing House
New Delhi - 110 002 (India)

UPPAL PUBLISHING HOUSE
3, Ansari Road, Daryaganj, New Delhi - 110 002
Phone: Off. 3273756, 3286571, Res. 2242884

William Carey Study and Research Centre
14/2 Sudder Street, Calcutta - 700 016
First Published 1997
ISBN 81-85565-81-3

Printed in India
Published by B.S. Uppal for UPPAL PUBLISHING HOUSE
3, Ansari Road, Darya Ganj, New Delhi - 110 002 and
Printed by Arora Offset Press, 817, Guru Ram Dass Nagar,
New Delhi - 110 092

PREFACE

This book is the maiden publication venture of the Subaltern Consultants Trust. The consultants are a group of people committed to the subaltern communities or sections, such as, the indigenous peoples, the dalits, the urban poor, and women. The tasks they have undertaken include documentation, studies, publications, consultations or conferences, and programmes of like nature.

The present volume is related to some of the effects of 'development' on tribal land, their displacement, and resettlement policies of the governments and public sector companies. The first section of the book, besides giving a brief historical background to the problem of alienation of land of the tribals, analyses several case studies in South Bihar. The stark reality of the socalled development reveals itself as a grim and disastrous process of dispossession or displacement of tribals and others in large numbers over several decades. The second part deals with the various resettlement policies for the displaced due to 'development' work and also contains a description of the people's reaction to some of these development projects.

One can approach these questions from two opposing perspectives. One, the NGO approach, is to take the fact of large-scale displacement for granted and then to look for suitable ways to resettle the displaced. The other, the movement approach, is to reject the very concept of the present development perspective and question the necessity of displacement. Both the parts of this book are inclined towards the latter perspective. They take the people's protests and movements, however sporadic, seriously and try to build up a strong case for alternatives to the present development process.

I hope this book will be of assistance to those who are engaged in tribal and dalit movements, and also to people interested in the subject.

Saral K. Chatterji
Hony. Director
William Carey Study and Research Centre

December 25, 1996
New Delhi - 110 014

CONTENTS

ALIENATION OF TRIBAL LAND IN JHARKHAND

A few case studies

S.Bosu Mullick

Introduction : The Issues

Cultural, social and in extension political identities of a people depend largely on the geographical area of its habitat. The ecology and environment of the land do not only shape the human nature and personalities of the members of the community but also provide a sense of belonging - an emotional attachment to the soil where they take birth, grow and pass away. The land provides sources of life, to live and to proliferate, offer natural resources to build society and thus becomes the arena of history of the community, ethnicity and nationality of human groups cannot be thought of in isolation of their land of habitation. The ancestry of an individual is traced not only through the lineage of the father or the mother but also along with the land of the ancestors and thus humanness is added to the physical land in terms of "father land" or "mother land" and "sons or daughters of the soil".

The role of land as the source of life as well as the identity of the people is more explicit and obvious in the case of the original settlers. Their relationship to land is much more deep rooted than those who settle later as emigrants. Often the second category of people tend to trace their origin in the land from where their ancestors migrated. Thus the nomenclature of the land and the original settlers are usually found to be the same.

Human relationship with land changes along with the social changes. In other words, with the evolution of the society different meaning and organising systems are also evolved with regard to land. Thus where as in the pristine society (pre-stratified society) the land mass of the globe was considered as "mother" with every human being having equal right on her, the stratified society emerged by condemning this very concept of "the mother earth" and thereby introducing the idea of land as private property. For the pristine society human relationship with land is not economic alone, land is life - both physical and spiritual. From this notion springs forth the wisdom of striking a balance between satisfaction of human's economic need and preservation of the physical nature for the emotional and psychological requirements of humankind. There is a sense of sharing the physical nature with the animal kingdom as well, because all living beings are considered to be the children of the "Mother Earth". The world outlook as it had involved in pristine society does negate any attempt to destroy nature to satisfy human greed but suggests the practice of taming nature for the benefit of the human collective*. Therefore, the wisdom of a judicial use of land for economic purpose and preservation of the rest is practiced. Land here is considered to be the gift of the supreme being for the common use. Human beings are supposed to enjoy usufructuary right over the land collectively. Individual ownership of land or exchange of it in lieu of any other thing is unimaginable in the pristine society. On the contrary, the stratified society, based on greed and individualism, competition and exploitation of man and women by man has reduced physical nature into a subject of exploitation. Land has been made a commodity. It is privatised and alienable. It has been made merely the subject of economic pursuit of man isolated from other social and spiritual considerations.

The contradiction between the two sets of value associated with land use is reflected in the historical contradiction between the pristine society and the "civilisation" (the highest stage of the development of stratified society). Ever since the birth of "civilisation" it has been snatching away the land belonging to the pristine society by invasion, subjugation and colonisation of the members of the latter. Desertification of all the early sites of "civilisation" is an eye opener to the fact of the

---

* Basu Mullick S. The intigrity of the Variegated creation : A Tribal point of view.
Religion and Society (Vol.XXXVII No.2 June. 1990 Bangalore) FN

destructive nature of the stratified society. Whether it is the salve-owning, feudal or capitalist form of society, "civilisation" with its insatiable greed has been aggressing upon the land protected and preserved for the generations to come by the people of the pristine society one after another leaving behind the dried bare skeleton of the earth far beyond the possibility of restoration.

The history of indigenous communities of Jharkhand has been woven around the central issue of their dispossession of the land inherited from their ancestors by the colonial forces through the ages. "It has also been the history of their stubborn resistance to the colonial onslaught of the Aryans and the Brahmanical Hindu states, Muslim invaders and the Mughal empire, East India Company and the British imperialism, and finally of the advanced nationalities and "internal-colonialsim" of the modern Indian state"[1]

The basic issue of the indigenous peoples of India and elsewhere in the world is that their identity is closely linked to the natural resources and the environment amidst which they live. They had developed cultural traditions and economy, social control mechanism, religious myths and techniques of production geared to retain this close link. Their cultural systems ensured that the resources continued to be their livelihood for several generations. They did this by using them judiciously to live on while at the same time ensuring their renewability. But today the mainstream society views their resources such as land and forest only as raw material to produce other consumer articles for the urban middle and upper classes. This society, therefore, tries to acquire monopoly over them. In the process control over these resources is transferred from the communities to whom this was a source of livelihood, to the corporate sector to which they are only a source of profit, and to the urban middle and

---

1. Bosu Mullick S. Jharkhand Movement Through Time, Religion and Society, Vol. XXXIII. No.3 & 4, September-December, 1991. pp.39.

upper classes to which it is one more raw material to cater to their consumer needs.

White colonisation of indigenous lands of the Amerindians in the Americas and those of the aboriginal populations of Australia and New Zealand was based on the assumption that they were "terra nullius" i.e. that they belonged to no one. As such "civilized population" had a right to occupy them. With the supreme court of Australia declaring in the Mabo case in 1993 that the principle of "terra nullius" cannot be recognised as valid anymore, the question of close link between the indigenous people and natural resources has been brought to the fore once again during the UN year of the indigenous peoples of the world.

In some form or the other, the same principle of "terra nullius" (referred to in this country as "eminent domain"), is applied in India to make it possible for the dominant classes to take control of these resources. In some cases it is used to take over land that was once under the control of the tribal communities, in others to displace people who have lived in a region for centuries though they might not have acquired the types of "patta" or land document required by the colonial law. In other cases it is used to take control of the forest from which they had traditionally got more than 50% of their food and had met most other needs. Thus the efforts of the dominant sections to control the natural resources, and the use they make of the principle of "eminent domain" have become basic to the life of the tribals also in India.

The principle of "eminent domain" is used in this case because much of the land the indigenous peoples have been living on, is considered as common property over which they have no right whatever according to the present legal system. For centuries they have survived in the informal society of a culture based on the word of mouth, legitimisation by the community and common property resource. The formal society, on the other hand, depends on the principle of a written document given to an individual. Property owned by an individual is basic to this economy.

One can thus see that the formal and informal systems belong to two different, even contradictory frameworks. What is called the common property resources has traditionally been the very basis of the indigenous people's economy. These resources belonged to the community and had to be treated as renewable. Individuals could use them only according to their needs and preserve them for posterity. The concept of individual or private property was not common among them. As a result of loss of control of the common property resources millions of indigenous persons have been displaced without any compensation. In the cases of the non-indigenous persons facing the same situation of displacement things are different because they have individual "pattas" and, therefore, entitled to receive compensation according to the market price of the land[2] .

The tribal communities of Jharkhand have their own meaning and organising system with regard to land including forest and water resources. All the spirits in their animistic belief system are protectors of land for the benefit of human beings. Their rights to the world along with the animal kingdom is inalienable. All land and forest under the usage of each village were considered as the common property resource before the invasion of the alien forces representing contradictory social systems. The new systems forcibly changed the traditional relationship between human and land. Major changes took place during the British colonial period. The British colonialism not only brought every inch of the tribal land under its control but also transformed the very nature of the CPR of every village. For the first time in the history of the people tribal lands were made private properties and the major portion of the tribal land was designated as the property of the government.

---

2 . Fernandez Walter An unpublished paper on Indigenous Peoples. 1993

Although Chotanagpur was ceded to the British in 1765 the first entry of the British into this region took place in 1772 when the Maharaja of Chotanagpur requested them to help him in a revenue matter. In 1780 the British established what was known as the Ramgarh Hill Tract. Chotanagpur was one of the areas under this administration. In 1793 the Permanent Settlement was introduced in Bengal and extended to Chotanagpur. In 1806 the Zamindari police system was established. The British started ruling the region indirectly through the Maharaja of Chotanagpur and the zamindars and their lackeys, all were aliens to the land. The gory story of the tribal people's struggle to protect their land and forest form the claws and the teeth of the "dikus" that followed needs no repetition here. Our concern is the outcome of the chain of tribal revolts that took place throughout the century. With a view to quell every rebellion the British came up with a compromising formula in terms of administrative reform and enactment of "protective land laws" in favour of the tribal communities.

The Tamar rebellion of 1789, 1797, 1807 and 1820 and finally the great "Koel Insurrection" of 1831 followed by the Bhumij rebellion of 1832 compelled the East India Company to come to an agreement with the people. But in the meantime the Maharaja and his gang destroyed the tribal land system. He acted as the absolute owner of the land of the tribals and fixed Royalities over the land and used to dispose it off at his sweet will. When the Company ended the indirect rule and took over the administration of the region in 1834 the tribal land system got broken all around. The British, instead of restoring the lost land to the tribals, took measures in the direction of total replacement of the old tribal land system and introduced a feudal relations of production in the land quite akin to their own in Europe.

All the so called protective laws that the British enacted from time to time to appease the rebellious tribal community turned out to be a process of legitimization of land alienated from the people for the benefit of the outsiders.

To summarise the history of the alienation of land belonging to the indigenous peoples of the then Chotanagpur since the beginning of the British rule in 1765 till the end of the 19th century no better word can possibly be used than those of Hofmann's : "The first ascertainable Jagir, i.e., grant of a village, made by hinduised rajas of Chotanagpur to one of the Hindu middlemen called into the country by them, is dated 1667. Up to that date every Mundari village had been in the full enjoyment of the rights, privileges and social and moral safeguards the race had laid down in the immemorial customs regulating the life of the village community. And now, in 1869 (the year of the passing of the Chotanagpur Tenure Act), it was found that in the 35 Paraganas alone, to which this settlement (Bhuinhair Survey and settlement) extended, 2,482 villages had lost all these rights and advantages, only comparatively few scraps of land being left to them as ancestral property. In the other paraganas things were not much better; and the last settlement (the survey and settlement which began on March 8th, 1902) of 1902 found in the whole of the estate under the Maharaja of Chotanagpur only 152 villages in the poorest parts of the province where there was little to rob, which still preserved the greater part of the ancient rights. The area within which these 152 villages lie, is hardly more than one percent of the Maharaja's estate. In 1765, just 98 years after the first grant to an alien, Chotanagpur fell under British Suzerainty together with Bihar, Bengal and Orissa; in 1772 Captain Camac led the first English force into the Palamu district and received the rajah of Chotanagpur as tributary chief. In 1806, the zamindari police, with Hindu zamindars darogas and aliens as chowkidars was introduced by the order of the E.I. Company, and in 1817 the country was brought under direct British administration. It is an undeniable fact that the years elapsing between 1805 and 1895 were the most fatal ones for the Mundas in particular and the aborigines in general.

The end of the British rule in India and the beginning of the sovereign nation-state of India in 1947 is marked by a more cruel, more overt and more calculated state aggression on the tribal society in India. After a long gory struggle during the British colonial rule the tribal societies finally succeeded in compelling the British Government to come to an agreement with them; and as a result of that a number of laws were enacted and arrangements were made to protect whatever little control the tribal societies retained in land till then. Atleast in theory the policy of protection of tribal rights on their habitat was accepted. Now, however, this was challenged by the ruling elite of independent India. While some anthropologists and social workers like Verier Elwin presented a policy of "isolation" of the tribals from the non-tribal society, the nationalists came out strongly, under their ideologue Prof. G.S. Ghurye, in favour of the theory of integration of society of the country. Finally, however, with the intervention of the Prime Minister, Pandit Jawahar Lal Nehru, the theory of "integration" was adopted by the state and constitutional arrangements were made accordingly2. This policy prompted the Government of India to ratify the International Labour Organisation's convention No.107 in 1957. But the events that followed proved beyond doubt that the policy practiced in reality was neither assimilation nor integration but that of "ethnocide". The tribal peoples in India were asked by the state to give up their claim to be the indigenous people of the country, and accordingly declared on the floor of the United Nations that India had no indigenous peoples3. The economic and cultural policies adopted by the state implied that all pre-modern forms of economic organisation must necessarily disappear to make way for either private or multi-national capitalism or state planned socialism or mixes thereof. In contravention to the spirit of the constitution of

---

2. Singh, K.S. Ethnicity and Development, Monohar, 1990.p.29

3. Jayant Prasad, Indian Permanent Mission to the United Nations, Geneva, 1987.

India the policy makers of the state accelerated this process by fast dispossessing the tribal people of their rights on land, water and forest in the name of "national interest" and "national development". The process of the alienation of tribal land in Chotanagpur should be seen in the light of these post-independence developments in the country.

The state has been proved to be the greatest tribal land grabber. Following the legacy of the previous colonial rules in the country the modern Indian state too has been depriving the tribal society of its traditional hold over the CPR to suit its economic needs and military requirements. The present ruling classes/castes of India, which remained powerless for more than five hundred years before independence in 1947 are now bent upon becoming rich and powerful within the quickest possible time. Therefore, instead of developing the quality of productive forces indigenously and changing the colonial relations of production, which is not only time taking but also painstaking they have chosen the easiest way of exploiting the natural resources indiscriminately to satisfy their greed. Most of the public sector industries are running at a loss but mining operations are registering tremendous profit. The cost benefit ratio of all the big dams meant for hydro-electric power generation shows the cost being much higher than the benefit. Inspite of that the state keeps constructing them to provide cheap power to the industries. It does so only to help Indian elites as well the middle class. Private contractors and traders are encouraged to thrive on the destruction of forests. The tribal society has been the worst victim of this greed of the ruling elites and the neo-rich of the post-colonial Indian society.

The dawn of the modern times in Chotanagpur set in with the construction of the "modern temples", to use the words of Pandit Jawahar Lal Nehru, in the form of big dams under Damodar Valley Corporation. The corporation displaced 93,487 persons from 84,140 acres of land destroying 305 villages mostly belonging to the tribals. Of these 37,320 acres were cultivable land[4]

Thus what was labeled as the "temple" turned out to be the graveyard of the tribals. And it was simply a humble beginning! What followed was a series of industries, mines, dams, urban centres and all sorts of allied establishments to cater to the needs of the outsiders who galloped into Chotanagpur in hordes and packs from all corners of the country, particularly from the plains of Bihar. The citation of a few of such projects would suffice the purpose of making this point. The Heavy Engineering Corporation Ltd. established at Hatia near Ranchi in 1958 displaced 12,990 persons from 9,22 acres of land from 46 villages which were acquired displacing 12,990 families. The Directory of Mines and Mine Leases, published in 1976 by the Indian Bureau of Mines, shows that there were about 300 mines operating in Singhbhum district alone and more than 1,51,000 acres of land were leased out, owned mostly by the private agencies. However, the total land area affected by mines is many times greater than the simple lease area. A rough estimate of the land alienated by the Uranium Corporation of India Ltd., at Jadugora in Singhbhum district amounts to 2,000 acres. The township of Jadugora is made out of five tribal villages. There is now a proposal of setting up a second nuclear fuel complex estimated to require around 300 acres of land. Under the Subarnarekha Multipurpose Project, for the construction of the two dams, two barrages, seven canals having a total length of 342 kms, 712 kms of roads, and for the construction of several colonies a vast area of tribal land is being acquired by the Government. For the Chandil dam alone 13,496,94 acres of land is needed. The Icha reservoir will cover 21,000 acres in Singhbhum and 10,500 acres in Orissa. The two canals from Icha will cover 58,700 acres in Singhbhum and 152,100 acres in Orissa. 10,000 acres of forest land is expected to be lost because of this project. In official

---

4. Singh Jagdish. Upper Domodar Valley : A study in settlement georgraphy. Inter
India publication, New Delhi 1985

reckoning, the Kutku dam in Palamau district would obliterate 14 villages. But the Chotanagpur Samaj Vikas Sanstha, an NGO fighting for the interest of the affected people, believes that more than 30 villages would be destroyed. According to the official estimate the dam when completed would submerge an area of 2,884 sq. kms. Out of the total submerged area of 20,000 acres about 13,000 acres are forest land and the rest is agricultural land. In Ranchi district alone, as per the information received from the Chief Engineer, Irrigation, Ranchi, there are about 44 complete irrigation projects and 21 incomplete ones. For the construction of only 10 such projects 5,135.73 acres of tribal land have been acquired. No information about the land acquired for the remaining 55 projects have been furnished. For the construction of the Koel-Karo Hydro Electric Project 50,000 acres of land will be needed, out of which 26,000 acres consist of cultivable land. The project will displace 66,000 people from 113 villages. The total mining activities in the North Karanpura valley under the CCL, according to the present estimate will cover 1,230 sq. kms. The Netarhat Field Firing range is going to acquire 1,471 sq. kms. There is no end to this kind of instances. And in every case people put up strong resistance. They were suppressed with strong hands of the state power, in many cases to the extent of killing them by police firing or by the hired criminals.

The state itself or in collusion with the individual land grabbers has been violating the so-called protective laws. Mr. F.A. Tailor, the settlement officer, after the Revisional survey which was carried out in the Ranchi district between 1927-37 observed: "The Tenancy Act (the Chotanagpur Tenancy Act, 1908) has not been an unqualified success in Ranchi district. As mentioned in the final report one of the chief objectives for which the CNT Act was introduced in 1908, was the protection of the more backward aboriginal clearers or tenants. But this object was not fully achieved. The professional money lenders succeeded in grabbing Tribal raiyati lands by ways of Zarpesgi, Bhugat-Bandha and auction purchases etc. In fact the CNT Act on the whole has been a failure as far as transfer in raiyati lands are concerned". Now in independent India it is not the money-lenders but, in the words of Mr. Bandi Oraon, Vice-chairman of the SC & ST Commission and also a member of the Bihar Legislative Assembly, "I have absolutely no hesitation in saying that...the Bihar Government, the entire machinery of the Bihar Government have been actively looting the lands and the lower Courts and the High Court have extended their support actively in this loot of tribal land making tribals landless and homeless and throwing a large number of them on the roads to take up the shameful job of begging".

Thus standing at the threshold of the 21st century a tribal person can see his or her further dispossession, degradation and finally total destruction in the coming century. Whereas for the non-tribal it is going to be an era of new hopes and prosperity, the proposed national policy for Rehabilitation of Persons Displaced as a consequence of Acquisition of Land clearly indicates a bleak future for the tribal peoples[5]. The details of this policy draft are dealt with in the next paper in this volume.

Indian ruling elites, with the help of the state have made the tribal peoples the worst victims of their own progress. They have adopted all possible means to dispossess them. Our general observations, supported and illustrated by the case studies, bring home the modus operandi. The following are the salient features of this operation.

1. Domestication of the tribal political leaders.
2. Rampant corruption in the bureaucracy, transfer of the well meaning officers from the tribal sub-plan areas.
3. Non dissemination of information to the affected people.

4. Overt disregard to the international agreements (ILO-107).
5. Blatant violation of Tribal Tenancy Acts.
6. Violation of the Constitutional Provisions (5th Schedule) by not forming or frustrating the Tribal Advisory Councils.
7. Imposition of Panchayat System in the schedule areas by dislodging the Tribal traditional political system.
8. Reluctance to formulate National Tribal Land Acquisition Policy.
9. Conspicuous absence of the national displacement and rehabilitation policy when tribal peoples are being displaced in thousands every year.
10. Shifting of funds allocated for tribal development to other accounts by the state governments.
11. Non acceptance of tribal traditional religious identity and entering them as Hindus in the Census Reports.
12. Snatching away the traditional rights of the society on forests.
13. Non acceptance of tribal people's rights on water resources.
14. Initiation of a rapid demographic change in the tribal areas by encouraging non-tribal people to settle there.
15. Complete disregard of environmental, archaeological and wild life issues.

The alienation of the tribal people from the national fabric has turned the cry of "national integration" and "national interests" into empty slogans for them. The under-estimation of the tribal unrest presently cropping up in a big way throughout the country will only add fuel to the fire of their dissociation from the Indian body polity the far reaching effect of which cannot be ignored. We should not forget that we are talking about more than 70 million people of our country. The phenomenon of alienation of tribal land is not just a localised issue. It had a past of blood and wounds, it has a present of frustration and beguilement and it will certainly have a disastrous consequence in future.

ALIENATION OF TRIBAL LAND IN THE URBAN AREA OF RANCHI

(A study of the situation of the tribal city-dwellers)

Not less than two thousand years ago, it is believed, different tribes of the Austro-Asiatic or Kolerian race started settling down in the plateau of Chutianagpur and adjacent Rajmahal hills. They developed an almost similar or parallel socio-religious complex, probably started germinating in their proto stage when they were one. In a later period the Uraons, a Dravidian speaking tribe, joined the Mundas. The term 'Sarna' or 'Sari' is referred to this system of belief. One of the salient features of the Sarna belief is its close relationship with nature. Nature in its concrete form in the Jharkhandi religious system has gradually assumed sublimity and has become abstract. Land, one of the chief components of Nature, is the very life source, the primary means of production of the tribes. Therefore, their attachment to and regard for it is manifested in their cultural practices. The Sarna is a holy grove, left untouched when a village was established by the symbol of nature. It is closely associated with his different religious practices. From his cradle to grave it is interlaced with almost each occasion of joy or sorrow of his life. The Masna is the place where he is buried after death. In the Akhra (dancing ground) he enjoys life with his fellows by dancing and singing. Each year he assembles on a particular ground called Jatra Tand along with other people of surrounding villages to demonstrate the military prowess of his race and political solidarity. Sometimes he goes to his "Buru" (festival), to propitiate the Bongas and to enjoy a gay musical night on that occasion. He has no idol to worship, no structure to put it in. The nature herself is the supreme power, he loves her, he fears her, he holds her in esteem. She needs no abode, no personification, she is physically present every where around him. He only selects certain parts of nature to mark her symbiotic presence and cherishes as much reverence for them as a Hindu does for his mandir (temple) idols or as a Christian does his church or the Holy Bible.

The city of Ranchi and its people

The name of the present city of Ranchi is a corrupt form of the village originally called the "Richi Hatu" after the hill "Richi Buru" under the foot of which it is situated. "Richi" means the Shikra, the bird of prey; "Buru" means hill and "hatu" stands for village. All these words are Mundari[2]. During the pre-British era the village "Chutia" was of some importance for trading and its old Hindu Mandir, now falls within the municipal area of Ranchi city, but not the Richi Hatu. With the establishment of the Cantonment in Doranda, meaning the "singing water", now called Doorang-da, and later the shifting of the office of

2. Ponette, P. Village Nomenclature of the Ranchi District, in Chotanagpur, ed. Bosu Mullick, S. opt. citd.p.68

the Commissioner of Chotanagpur to Ranchi from Lohardaga, Ranchi emerged as an important place in the political map of the British occupied Chotanagpur. As a consequence outsiders started settling down in Ranchi. The tiny village Richi hatu and other small neighbouring villages, such as, Hehal (large purple creeper), Hesel (straight large tree with whitish bark), Hesag (tree of the Ficus family), Hinoo (Hinua, lapwing, bird of the plover family), Kadru (large climber), Harmu (the pagolin, scaled ant-eater), Chutia (field mouse), Kokar (owl), Piska (common creeper), Tiril (Indian ebony tree), etc.[3], gradually got knitted together as one town. Though Ranchi Municipality was constituted in 1869 and it was declared as town in 1872, the tribal character of the place was still visible. However, with the consolidation of the British rule in Jharkhand with its seat of the region in Ranchi the presence of the aliens became quite conspicuous very soon. By the turn of the century the population of the town was about 26 thousand which was doubled by 1931. The immediate reason of this growth was immigration of population from outside the district as was rightly observed by Mr. Taylor, the Settlement Officer, in 1935, "In Ranchi and Lohardaga, particularly the former, there are many outside elements from other parts of India. In Ranchi town Bengalis form the majority of the intruders......Biharis are also well represented in Ranchi and Lohardaga towns. The landlord class in the District contains many Biharis and a smaller number of Bengalis. The professional money lending class is still almost entirely Biharis and Bengalis..... Out of the present population of the district 15;67,149 (according to census

---

3. ibid,p.66-68

report tribal population was 9,12,865 and non-tribals were 6,54,284) as compared to 1901 census the Hindus increased by 83%, Christian 110% and Mohammedans by 34%. Animists have during this period decreased by 33%" 4 One of the minor reasons of this decrease might be the conversion of a section of the tribal population into Christianity and a few of them remaining as Hindus and secondly, a large scale emigration of tribals to the tea gardens of Assam owing to the failure of the harvest in 1918. During the last few years of the British rule the population increase was nominal, but immediately after independence in 1947 it registered a phenomenal increase and continued to be so in the following decades. The following Table-I gives us the true picture of this abnormal growth of population in the city of Ranchi.

Table - I

	1881		1891	
	Population	% increase	Population	% increase
Ranchi urban agglomeration	18,443		20,396	10.01
	1901		1911	
	Population	% increase	Population	% increase
	25,970	27.89	32,994	27.05
	1921		1931	
	Population	% increase	Population	% increase
	39,628	20.11	50,517	27.48

---

4. Taylor, F.E.A. Settlement Officer, Final Report on the Revisional Survey and Settlement Operation in the District of Ranchi (1927-350) Government Printing Press, Bihar, Patna. 1940.pp.4-5.

1941		1951	
Population	% increase	Population	% increase
62,562	23.84	106,849	70.79
1961		1971	
Population	% increase	Population	% increase
140,253	31.26	266,545	90.05
1981		1991	
Population	% increase	Population	% increase
502,771	88.63	599,306	19.02

Massive industrialization implies expansion of existing small towns and establishment of new townships. But in Chutinagpur, in general this has been deterred by the very nature of the acts regarding land transaction on the one hand and by the unplanned and unwise attitude of the Govt. on the other. Chotanagpur Tenancy Act (1908) and Santhal pargana Tenancy (Supplementary provisions) Act (1949) ban alienation of tribal land without prior permission of the District Commissioner. Moreover the Scheduled Areas Regulations (1969) are supposed to deal with the problems of land alienation and restoration of alienated tribal land, which is applicable to the entire scheduled areas. The Govt. has developed a great credibility gap between itself and the tribal people by displacing them with promises during the setting-up of industries which it did not fulfil properly. Even the compensation paid to the displaced people was so meagre and whimsical that they were not enabled to resettle themselves. These instances have made the tribal land owners very much reluctant to part with land for Govt. projects on housing or other related schemes. Nevertheless, towns grew into cities and village and rich cultivable lands turned into towns in an utterly haphazard manner. And still this process is being continued. But all at the cost of local people's belief, tradition and legal rights.

Present urban Ranchi, with its industries and booming market, developed centering old Ranchi town, into a glaring example of rapid urbanisation initiated by the independent Govt. of India. It has extended itself from Dhurwa (HEC) to Kanke and from Tatisilway to Hehal, an area, only thirty years back, excluding the tiny town of Ranchi was chiefly rural in nature, full of small villages though scattered but socio-politically closely knitted. The population consisted of tribes like the Mundas, the Oraons, some Hindu late settlers called the sadans and some Muslim converts as well as a few outsiders. Though Ranchi Municipality was constituted in 1869 and it was declared as a town in 1872 at that time Ranchi town was chiefly known to the outsiders as a health resort, with a cantonment and some Govt. offices, a place of forest and local trade. The jurisdiction of the Municipality was only 6 sq. miles in 1917. It became 12.39 sq. miles in 1971. The population was only 33,069 in 1911 which rose to 122.461 in 1961. In 1971 census report it was recorded to be 1,75,934. With the wave of industrialization in the 50s Ranchi became a booming city thickly populated and suffering from acute housing and sanitation problems.

Surrounding villages lost their tribal flavour by the pressure of the new settlers. Legally transactionable land registered an incredible price rise but that was also too meager to accommodate the new comers. Illegal transaction of land reached great heights.

With the passage of time and accumulation of wealth by the new comers, who enjoyed the lion share of the wealth generated by industry and trade, the demand for land increased conspicuously. As a result the price of a Katta of transactional land in Burdwan Compound area rose to Rs.3,000/- in 1975 from Rs.600/- in 1952; and in 1982 it was Rs.18,000/- Now it is more than a lakh. In Hindpiri, a non-posh area, it was only Rs.2,000/- to Rs.3,000/- in 1977. It increased to Rs.10,000/- per katta in 1985 and now it is Rs.35,000/-. Similarly in Pepee Compound area a piece of land which was bough at Rs.300/- per katta only 15 years back is now being sold at Rs.1,15,000/- or above. The dearness and non-availability of land and consequent awful housing problems have given birth to a tendency of encroaching adjacent vacant land among the people who have already managed to occupy some landed property, and at the same time a trend of grabbing vacant land by any means among the land hungry new comers. These cases of intrusions, encroachments or trespassing are chiefly being faced by the tribal owners. In some cases this has also happened to the vested lands owned by the government. In this context the plight of the tribal people in and around the city demands a brief discussion. In a word, the social status of the tribes in relation to the aliens, in the changed situation, has been degraded to a great extent. Industry, trade, administration, communication media, all are dominated by outsiders. Therefore, they are far more affluent and powerful than the local tribal populace. The former developed an island of their own, detached socially, culturally and racially from the surrounding tribal world; while the latter is living a ghetto life in utter poverty and degradation neglected by the government, suppressed and abused by the alien neighbours.

However, the tribal city dwellers, or rather those who were compelled to live in the city, are also ignored and looked down upon by their own brethren who are economically well off and well established in the changed social situation. The tribal elite and the middle class have almost totally abandoned their traditions and are vigorously trying to fit themselves into the order of the day, rubbing shoulders with their alien counterparts. Only the poor tribal people are still unable to sever their attachment with the tradition. But having been afflicted by hatred and lured by money either they have shrunk into their individual selves or have fallen into self-destruction and moral degradation. In the city 99% of the slums were once tribal villages. Gradually being pressed from all corners they have become the black spots on the "beautiful" face of affluent Ranchi. Loosing cultivable lands, either by illegal sale at a very low price or by encroachments most of the families have let their members work as daily labourers, rickshaw pullers or menials. Unemployed youngsters have turned into street corner delinquents. The traditional economic order has been devastated and in the new order they have not found any place. Abnormal consumption of country liquor, increasing participation in gambling, involvement in antisocial activities are some of the symptoms of their social and cultural degeneration. Moreover, the contra-cultural effect of commercial Hindi films, cultural forms of outsiders, have been changing their world outlook, particularly as concerns exploitation of women. Against this current only a few conscious people remain in these slums who follow their traditions and belief. The intruders and the land grabbers understand this weakness of the tribals and accordingly take advantage of it. Table 2 gives us an estimate of the slums in the city of Ranchi.

Table - 2

TOWN DIRECTORY

STATEMENT - IV: A Civic and Other Amenities in Notified Slums, 1979

Name of Slum	Area of slum (in sq. kms.)	Population of slum
Argora	0.029	3,600
Barhi Toli	0.06	650
Bariyatu	0.26	1,500
Chadri	0.03	400
Chuna Bhatta	0.12	480
Darji Mohalla	0.12	3,000
Dom Toli	0.13	5,000
Dom Toli	0.06	600
Dhamsa Toli	0.13	300
Gari Toli	0.51	700

Gonda Hatma	0.25	6,000
H'arijan Toli (Kasai Mohalla)	0.15	1,200
Harmu Tola	0.29	3,000
Hessel (back of Bank Colony)	0.62	500
Irgu Tola	0.32	800
Kadru	0.23	900
Karam Toli	0.10	1,000
Khorha Toli	0.08	900
Kumhar Toli (Kasai Mohalla)	0.23	1,200
Kumhar Toli (Ward No.17)	0.06	900
Kusa Toli	0.13	1,000
Lac Factory Area (Hindpiri)	0.13	5,000
Lowadih	0.06	1,150
Lower Chutia	0.13	400
Madhukam	0.19	2,500
Mani Toli (Doranda)	0.06	1,200
Mochi Toli (Doranda)	0.06	1,000
Morhabadi	0.20	3,200
Nagra Toli	0.27	8,000
Pathal Kudwa	0.23	2,500
Purani Ranchi	0.13	600
Sarmlong	0.14	2,200
Tamtam Toli	0.13	300
Tunki Toli	0.17	350
Upper Chutia	0.13	600
TOTAL		**62,630**

Encroachment and illegal occupation of land having socio-religious significance.

Within the jurisdiction of Ranchi municipality there are five kinds of communally owned land, associated with the socio-religious practices of the local tribal people, which have been encroached or forcibly occupied without having any legal grounds by both private and government agencies, by individuals or groups. These types of land are the Sarna, the Jatra Tand, the Masna, the Khalihans and the pahanai land. During the period of the last settlement which was completed in 1925, communally owned landed properties except Pahanai land were recorded as vested land because nobody, quite naturally, claimed an individual right to them. Later on, it seems, on demand placed by the people in some records a special reference was added pointing out the nature of the land as Sarna, Masna and so on. Thus the right of the community was not firmly established on these lands. However, no one bothered about this legal matter because until the beginning of industrialisation in the 50s the demand for land was negligible and the question of encroachment did not arise. In settlement records Pahanai land offered conditionally by the village council (parha or pati) to the Pahan to meet religious expenses was not vested because the pahans claimed their rights to them. However, in tradition the pahanship is not a hereditary post, therefore, the pahanai land cannot be the private property of the Pahan. But in settlement records it was shown so because of the ignorance of the officials. Presently, in many cases, particularly in urban areas where the traditional social structure has become weakened or even broken down the Pahans are capitalising on this mistake in records and posing as the sole proprietors of the land. In some cases the pahanai land has been partitioned legally among the sons of a deceased Pahan.

Even after independence the government officials, chiefly non-tribals, neglected this issue and treated those communally owned plots as government vested lands. Naturally where the tribal people opposed this sharp conflict arose between them and the government resulting in nothing but the maintenance of status quo.

In the course of my study I have come across 8 typical cases of this type of land alienation occurring within Ranchi municipal area.

1. In Misir Gonda the Sarna land has been encroached by a non-tribal individual who constructed a part of his house on it.
2. In Karamtola, the khalihan land was occupied by a group of Punjabis in order to erect a home for handicapped persons eventually restored by the villagers after a prolonged struggle.
3. In Chandri, the Jata land has been occupied by the municipality itself and staff quarters have been constructed on it.
4. In the same village, the Sarna land has been encroached partly by the owner of a cinema hall.
5. In Nagratoli, the Masna land has been occupied by a Hindu temple and adjacent house of the priest and partly the cowsheds of the non-tribal milkmen.
6. In Kokar, Jatra land has been encroached by individuals, fake committees of so called social workers and temples.
7. The Sarna of the same village has been partly occupied by the erection of a Hindu temple.
8. In Hindpiri, Pahanai land has been sold to the individuals by the Pahan himself. The Masna of the same village was also sold by him but eventually restored.

In all these cases the government agencies remained either indifferent to the tribal people or helped directly or indirectly the land grabbers. It is reported that bribing petty officials in local police stations some times played a great role in the cases of encroachment by individuals. Religious sentiments, often fanatic, of the administrative officials, mostly Hindus, were exploited in case of land grabbing by erecting temples. Political lobbying was done in the cases of grabbing under the banner of social work. Slogans, like "the interest of the nation should be regarded as greater than that of community", were raised in cases of land grabbing by the municipality. And in all cases "the specter of communal tension" haunted the higher administrative officials whenever protest by the tribal populace occurred. Moreover, the land grabbers, in general, enjoyed overt support from their respective caste-fellows and were never opposed by the non-tribal communities as a group.

The tribal people on the other hand, never received justice, in any one of the cases studied, from the administration. Tribal elites of the town never stood actively behind the culturally oppressed villagers. Christian tribals remained altogether indifferent to these impropriety. Political parties never came forward to take up the just causes. Press, in general, except one English weekly, The New Republic (now closed down), never published the truth. Relative isolation of the tribal city dwellers from their brethren in the countryside seems to be the reason for lack of mass protest. These cases also reveal the inherent socio-cultural weakness in concerned tribal people. Weak or no longer existing traditional social institutions, feeble ties to their traditional religion, consequent moral degradation, inferiority complex and poverty are the major causes of the city tribals, inability to respond aggressively to the challenge of the land grabbers.

Tribal lands grabbed for housing purposes

In and around the urban area of Ranchi a huge quantity of land belonging to the tribal people have been transacted both legally and illegally by the government of Bihar and handed over to the non-tribal outsiders for housing and other private purposes. Mr. Bandi Oraon, M.L.A. and the Vice-Chairman of the SC and ST Commission, pointed out some of the outstanding cases.

Bihar State Housing Board

The State Government acquired about 500 acres of first class agricultural land, mostly of the Adivasis, and handed it over to the Bihar State Housing Board against the will of the owners. The Board constructed houses of different types in Harmu, Argora and Bariatu and allotted them to mostly the Biharis. The Board transferred about 165 acres of land to the Ashok Nagar Housing Cooperative where palatial buildings were erected by the moneyed outsiders.

A.G. Office Housing Cooperative Society

The Bihar Government acquired about 75 acres of 1st class agricultural land, falsely showing as barren, in Kadru by turning a deaf ear to the continuous protest of the Adivasi owners. The land was taken in two lots. During the acquisition of the second lot on 8th March, 1983 there was literally a pitched battle between the administration headed by all the outsiders armed with heavy police force and the Adivasis. The acquisition was illegal according to the ruling of the Bombay High Court which gave a verdict that Housing Societies did not come under the purview of the "public purposes". The purpose of the acquisition was to build houses for the employees of the Accountant General's office situated in Doranda, also on the Adivasi land. The Housing Cooperative consisted of members who were overwhelmingly from outside Chotanagpur numbering 800 odd persons. Some of them were not even the employees of A.G. Office. Some I.A.S. and I.P.S. officers were also rewarded with one plot each free of cost. Other non-A.G. employees who got their share in the loot were physicians, engineers, Block Development Officers, Circle Officers, politicians including one former Member of the Bihar Legislative Assembly etc., all hailing from outside Chotanagpur. The Cooperative paid about Rs.500 (five hundred) per decimal as compensation and sold it to the non A.G. employees at the rate of 30 to 40 thousand rupees per decimal. All efforts to draw the attention of the Government of Bihar proved to be futile. A number of such housing cooperatives are still coming up in and around the city of Ranchi on the tribal land measuring thousands of acres.

Case Study 2

COAL MINING : Parej East and Piparwar Open Cast Projects.

The richness of the land of Jharkhand in minerals, particularly of the Chotanagpur division has been the source of greatest misfortune for the tribal people of the region. The deadly claw of the modern civilisation with its five sharp nails of mining, power generation, indutrialisation, urbanisation and deforestation has torn "mother earth" apart dispossessing the people of their land. The mining operations have proved to be the most disastrous.

Though the region is littered with mines of all sorts, eg. iron, coal, copper, bauxite, mica, limestone, chromite, manganese, uranium etc. coal mining has been the oldest and largest among them all. According to recent estimates 44.12 percent of the total coal reserves in the country lie in Jharkhand[5], and its contribution to the country's 200 mts. coal production is 60%[6] . Coal is found in the Gondwana rocks of the Damodar basin. The well known coalfields of the area are Raniganj, Jharia, East and West Bokaro, Ramgarh, South and North Karanpura. The smaller mines of Deogarh, Daltonganj, Hutar, Auranga and Rajmahal coalfields are situated to the north of the main Gondwana basin.

The establishment of the first coal mine in Raniganj dates back to the year 1774. The first joint stock company M/s. Bengal Coal Company was formed in the year 1843.

---

5. Areeparampil, Mathew.1995. Displacement Due to Mining in Jharkhand (unpublished)

6. Baliga, P. and S. Shekkhar. "Need for Establishing 'Coal Institute for Environment and Occupational Health', paper presented at the workshop on "Concern and Care for Environment", Ranchi, organised by Coal Mining, Planning and Design Institute Ltd. (CMPDIL) 199,p.14.

After this a chain of collieries were established on the left bank of the Damodar river. The working of Jharia, Bokaro and Karanpura coalfields started in 1856. The opening of coal mining in Dhanbad area during the second half of the 19th century and the establishment of the Tata Iron and Steel Company in Jamshedpur in 1907 marked the beginning of the large scale exploitation of minerals and other resources of this area[7]. Prior to 1970-71 coal was mined in haphazard manner by private mine owners. After the nationalisation of coking coal in 1971 and non-coking coal in 1973 the entire coal industry of the region was entrusted to Coal India Ltd. (CIL) and its subsidiaries excepting a few captive mines of ISCO, IISCO and DVC. Coal India owns and operates 494 (in Jharkhand region 189) mines and 15 coal washeries through its subsidiary companies. The subsidiary companies are :

i. Bharat Coking Ltd. (BCCL) has in its charge 390 nationalised mines and moondih mines which were earlier owned by the NCDC.

ii. Eastern Coalfields Ltd. (CL) covers the Raniganj coalfieds in West Bengal and Mugma, Rajmahal coalfields in Bihar.

iii. Central Coalfields (CCL) covers the Bokaro, Ramgarh, Giridih and North and South Karanpura coalfields in Bihar, the Talcher coalfields in Orissa and Singrauli coalfields, in M.P. and U.P. The company owns 57 coal mines, 4 coal washeries and a by-product coke plant.

Coal is India's most important source of commercial energy providing two-thirds of India's energy needs. Faced with a rapidly growing energy demand,

---

7. Areeparampil, Mathew. Industries, Mines and Dispossession. In Developmnt Displacement and Rehabilitation.Ed. by Fernandes. Walter and Thukral, Enakshi Ganguly. Indian Social Institute, 1989.p.16.

small reserves of hydrocarbons and steeply rising costs of developing its hydroelectric resources, India relies heavily on its abundant coal output which is used to generate electricity. 15% produces steel, and 25% in industrial plants (cement, fertilizer, etc., to fuel boilers, Coal India Limited (Coal India) produces about 90% of the coal output.

In 1991-92 Coal India earned a profit of Rs.167 crores. Nationalisation of coal has resulted in a dramatic increase in coal output. From a mere 72.95 Mt. in 1970-71 coal production has quadrupled to around 305 Mt. per annum today. It is poised to touch 417 Mt. by the year 2000 A.D. Over 60 percent of this expected to come from open cast is mining. The production of CCL is estimated to increase from 29.25 mts. in 1990-91 to 67.00 mts. in 1999-2000[8].

The Coal India is at present acquiring extensive land areas and displacing a large number of families. According to an estimate, between 1981 and 1985 the Central Coalfields Ltd. has acquired 1,20,300 acres of land. Similarly Eastern Coalfields has acquired about 30,000 acres during the Sixth Plan period. More than 32,750 families have been displaced. But Coal India could offer jobs only to 11,901 displaced persons[9].

Table I :

Number of families displaced and number of jobs provided by CIL

---

8. Tandon, G.L. "Scenario of Environmental Status in Coal Mining in India" in Dhar, B.B. Environment Managemnt of Mining Operations. New Delhi, Ashis Publishing House. 1990.pp.17-57

9. Singh, V.K. "Environmental Management vis-a-vis Mineral Development",
parer present at workshop on "Concern and Care for Environment", Ranchi, organised by CMPDIL. 1991,p.2

S.No,	Company	No. of families Displaced	No. of jobs provided to one member of the family
1.	Eastern Coalfields Ltd.	14,750	4,915
2.	Central Coalfields Ltd.	7,928	3,984
3.	Western Coalfields Ltd.	6,232	2,250
4.	Bharat Coking Coal Ltd.	3,841	750
	TOTAL	**32,75**	**11,901**

(Source: Govt. of India, 1985)

A study made by the CMPDI has indicated that till 1994-95 the total land requirement for coal projects in Jharkhand area would be 62,642 hectares (156605 acres) of which 22,843 ha (57,107.5 acres) i.e. 37% would be forest land. Out of this 11,909 hactares of forest land and 26,576 hactares of non-forest land would be taken up by coal projects in Karanpura valley alone[10]. The Rajmahal Coal Mining Project of ECL in the Godda district will displace about 6,000 people from seven villages. In this project the pit area under proposed mining covers 5.5 sq.kms. The Piparwar Coal project, located in the North Karanpura valley, covers an area of 6.38 sq.kms, with minable coal reserves of 197 million tonnes. According to official claims the project will displace 460 families from two villages. However, unofficial reports say that at least 15,000 people from 14 villages and hamlets will be severely affected by the mines, the washery and other auxiliaries .

---

10. Singh, J. 1985. Upper Damodar Valley : A Study in Settlement Georgraphy. New
Delhi : Inter-India Publications.pp.223.

Caste study - 2:1

Parej East Open Cast Project

Introduction

Today's Damodar valley and the surrounding region, best known to the "civilised" world for its Damodar Valley Corporation and its barrages, "the modern temple of the independent India", and the glorious coalfields, was called Chain Champa. Even the early geographical maps prepared by the British East India Company after its occupation of the region maintained this ancient name. According to the Santhal mythology the Kherowars after being defeated in Kadaligarh migrated to Chain Champa and settled there. In the heart of the region is the much revered Lugu Buru , the Lugu hill. "Under its foot our foreparents evolved the Dang Serng (the Dang dance form and accompanying music)", say the Santhals. Then came the famine along with the British. Under the Zamindari operation the Santhals got restless. Lured by the British a large number of them migrated to Damin-i-koh (the Santhal Paraganas). The Dikus took over the land reclaimed and made cultivable by the Santhals. The dense forest was denuded. Throughout the British colonial period the Santhals and other minor tribes including the Birhors kept losing their control over the land and the forest. In independent India if the DVC came in as the death blow to the tribal people of the region the coal mines are coming up as the graveyards of the dead. The DVC alone had displaced 93,874 persons from 84,140 acres of land from 305 villages. Of these 37,320 acres were cultivated[12] . The Lugu hills stand between East and West Bokaro coalfields. The West Bokaro Coalfields cover an area of 207 sq. kms. with 19 mines in operation at present. The private coal mines of the Tata Iron and Steel Company (TISCO) are also situated in this area.

---

12. Tandon, G.L. ibid.pp.29

The Parej East Open Cast Project is located in the West Bokaro Coalfields, which comes under the Central Coalfields Ltd., a subsidiary of the Coal India Ltd. A total of 4.6 billion tonnes of coal reserves has been estimated in the West Bokaro coalfields of which about 4.4 billion tonnes are coking.

The coal reserves are confined upto a depth of 300 meters. The 19 mines which are in operation at present produce around 3.5 million tonnes of coal per annum. The major portion of it (2.6 million tonnes) comes from the open cast mines.

The Parej East Open Cast Project is being financed by the World Bank. It carries a coal reserve of 41.45 million tonnes with a life span of 27 years. The project has grade IV washery coal. "A capital investment of Rs.16.5 crores had been made and so far 4400 tonnes of coal have been extracted from Parej", reveals Mr. M.P. Mishra, General Manager, CCL. He further adds that it is an open cast mine with an output of 1.75 million tonnes per year.

Displacement and Rehabilitation

According to the 1st notification issued in 1987 the land which was to be immediately acquired amounted to 1350 acres from the villages Durukasmar, Ulhara and Barisom. The Pindara Block was chosen for rehabilitation of the displaced people. According to the present estimate for the first 10 years of mining 323.45 ha of land will be required. It has been further estimated that for the full life operation of the mines under the project another 427.61 ha of land would be acquired. The geographical area of the forest land, tenancy land and government land has been worked out to be 86.80 ha, 24.92 ha and 211.73 ha respectively for the first 10 years of operation.

The following table shows the number of house oustees.

Villages	House oustees			
	SC	ST	Others	Total
Parej	60	71	100	231
Durukasmar	70	92	57	219
Barughutu	43	45	57	145
TOTAL	**173**	**208**	**214**	**595**

The rehabilitation and resettlement policy makes provisions for one job for every two acres of irrigated land and one job for every three acres of un-irrigated land. Compensation in terms of provision of employment only takes into account land owners and persons not owning land are left out. This latter group includes sharecroppers, tenants, land squatters and agricultural labourers. In the matter of compensation there arises a number of problems. First of all, those who do not have ownership patta are not entitled to receive any compensation. Now there are many tribal families who do not have the patta because they cultivate "Gair Majurwa" (legally owned by the govt.) land. They have so far been denied the patta though the land has been under their possession for last three generations. It was observed that in many cases the land oustees did not receive the full amount of compensation. Even if the money was deposited in the bank in the name of the land oustees the middlemen take a share when the money is withdrawn from the bank. On the matter of employment the management talks of labour surplus and hence no recruitment takes place; but at the same time it is found that labourers are being recruited from outside the region.

Population

Table I and II present 1971 and 1991 population figures of two panchyats namely Tapin and Banji. There are altogether 12 villages present in these two panchayats.

The number of collieries present in Tapin and Banji panchayats are altogether six, namely :-

I. *TAPIN PANCHAYAT*

1. Tapin Block or Colliery
2. Pindra Block (Proposed Rehabilitation Site)
3. Parej Block

II. *BANJI PANCHAYAT*

1. Burughutu Block
2. Kotra Block
3. Basantpur Block

All the above mentioned collieries fall under West Bokaro Coalfields. It has many more collieries present in the whole area.

A closer look at the population figures reveals a changing pattern of Tribal and Non Tribal population. The twelve villages which we have noted, the Scheduled Tribe population was 18.30% of total population in 1971. The number decreased to 11.68% of total population in 1991. On the other hand, the general population and the Scheduled Caste population which were 70.03% and 11.67% respectively of total population in 1971 rose upto 73.09 and 15.23 of the total population in 1991.

The trend of population has migratory pattern which tells us that the opening of collieries have pulled in the non-tribals from nearby areas and from other districts of Bihar in search of employment and other economic gains. Whereas the autochthonous inhabitants are getting pushed out or dispersed. The new class of people comprises of Thikedars, Dalals, Entrepreneurs, Shop Vendors (informal sectors) and employees of public and private sectors like CCL and TISCO.

Thus, the opening of collieries have been acting adversely for the tribal population in terms of employment or job absorption. Few of the tribals who have succeeded in getting jobs mainly remain as blue collared workers. The actual needy person in want of a job never gets it.

Second aspect of Collieries and Mining have been an increased pressure on land and forests. The increased mining has led to cultivators losing their land to government for mining operations and also to outsiders who remain as entrepreneurs. Land and forests, main source of livelihood of the tribal people have either been snatched away or very little of it has remained. The leasehold boundary acts as a danger line for them.

The ascendance in the numerical proportion of non-tribals have resulted into divides, bickering and factionalism based on ethnic regional and class considerations. The population increase and the scarcity related to economic and social needs, an interpolation of facts, leads to extrapolating the fear of what might happen to the next generation.

Ecological Dimensions

Earlier history indicates that the valley remained mostly dominated by the tribals, mainly Santhals. It is only after the mining operations began that major changes have occurred and the whole setting has been transformed. Impact of mining is briefly considered under its various components or dimensions.

The ecological ties which the tribals have with land, nature and forest need hardly to be stressed. For the tribals, the trinity is not just their means of survival but around these their whole life revolves. The place is rich in flora and fauna. Its flora is composed of Nim. Khairwa, Palas, Bel, Anula. Mango, Sahtoot, Jamun, Karam, Mahua etc. The fauna consists of leopards, wolves, deer, hyena, sambhar, wild bears, rabbits. But wild life has started decreasing in recent days. The forest provides fuel wood, timber and medicines.

As soon as one enters the valley, one can immediately hear the noise of the drill, dumpers and other equipments busy in their tasks of digging and unloading excavated materials for trying to reach the seamy layers of sedimentary rocks commonly known as coal. Tragically one coal mine may have many removals of top soil further ahead depending on the availability of coal. The process virtually leaves big excavated areas. The result is a total destruction of natural vegetation in and around the place. The air most of the time remains loaded with coal dust. The washery remains a place no less inundated with the waste products of coal mining operations making the river too dirty resulting in all kinds of pollution.

The impact of mining has many other dimensions too. The blasting operations leaves deep cracks in the walls of mud houses. There is always an increased fear for villagers to be caught unaware and become victims of blasting while on their way to natur's call.

When we try to look into environmental hazards we find that they are numerous. The mining activities leave behind :

1. Coal dust
2. Washery effluent
3. Generation of overburden
4. Gaseous emission
5. Destruction of flora and fauna

Cultural Dimensions

The changes in the physical environment and in the social setting have a profound impact on the cultural and religious traditions of the tribal population. For the tribals the place of worship is the Sarna, the sacred grove. In some villages the Sarna has been acquired for mining operations. All tribal religious festivals like Karma and Sarhul, are directly related with nature and the forests. As the forests are disappearing the tribals also have lost their cultural roots. With the influx of outsiders into the area and the local communities being displaced, the moral values of the tribal community are destroyed and they become corrupt and start exploiting their own people.

It is not uncommon for an outsider (Diku) to keep a tribal woman as his concubine. In traditional tribal society social sanctions would have prevented such happening but today the traditional panchayat system has broken down and as a result tribal values are on the decline.

In Parej it can be seen that hundreds of trucks are lined up along the road for loading. As there are long lines the truck drivers go and visit the nearby settlements to pass the time. Regular cases of rape occur and some of the grass-root social workers feel that the much feared AIDS disease may spread to this area.

TABLE I. 1971 CENSUS FIGURES

PANCHAYAT TAPIN	SCHEDULED TRIBE %	SCHEDULED CASTE %	GENERAL	TOTAL
1. TAPIN	149(23.35)	151(23.67)	338(52.98)	638(100.00)
2. RAUTA	68(37.37)	13(7.14)	101(55.49)	182(100.00)
3. PINDRA	109(55.61)	10(5.10)	77(39.29)	196(100.00)
4. ULHARA	127(100.00)	NIL	NIL	127(100.00)
5. BARISAM	134(100.00)	NIL	NIL	134(100.00)
6. PAREJ	98(27.92)	117(33.33)	136(38.75)	351(100.00)
7. DURUKASMAR	197(39.56)	128(25.70)	173(34.74)	498(100.00)
PANCHAYAT BANJI				
8. BANJI	136(17.53)	193(24.57)	447(57.60)	776(100.00)
9. BURUGHUTU	958(12.62)	667(8.78)	5970(78.60)	7595(100.00)
10. KOTRE		UNINHABITED		

11. PANCHANDA	NIL	01(0.46)	218(99.54)	219(100.00)
12. BASANTPUR	123(16.32)	58(7.69)	573(75.99)	754(100.00)
TOTAL	2099(18.30)	1338(11.67)	8033(70.03)	

11470(100.00)

TABLE II. 1991 CENSUS FIGURES

PANCHAYAT	SCHEDULED	SCHEDULED	GENERAL	TOTAL
TAPIN	TRIBE %	CASTE %		
1. TAPIN	488(20.54)	598(25.17)	1290(54.29)	2376(100.00)
2. RAUTA	124(38.04)	12(3.68)	190(58.28)	326(100.00)
3. PINDRA	279(16.71)	245(14.67)	1146(68.62)	1670(100.00)
4. ULHARA	179(93.23)	5(2.60)	8(14.17)	192(100.00)
5. BARISAM	157(78.11)	29(14.42)	15(7.47)	134(100.00)
6. PAREJ	240(16.90)	322(21.58)	930(62.33)	1492(100.00)
7. DURUKASMAR	649(49.29)	236(17.92)	432(32.80)	1317(100.00)
PANCHAYAT BANJI				
8. BANJI	142(12.62)	532(47.29	451(40.09)	1125(100.00)
9. BURUGHUTU	870(5.21)	2093(12.55)	13723(82.24)	16686(100.00)
10. KOTRE		UNINHABITED		
11. PANCHANDA	4(0.73)	10(1.82)	536(97.45)	550(100.00)
12. BASANTPUR	44(3.51)	58(4.62)	1152(91.87)	1254(100.00)
TOTAL	3176(11.68)	4140(15.23)	19873(73.09)	27189(100.00)

(Data collected by the research wing of the Xavier Institute of Social Service)

Case Study - 3

Coal Mining in North Karanpura Basin : Piperwar Opencast Project

Of late the world's largest opencast coal mining project in the North Karanpura Valley has drawn the attention of not only the concerned people and press in India but also that of the world community. We are overwhelmed by the sheer magnitude of the project covering an area of 1230 sq. kms. The number of people to be displaced will go into tens of thousands and the number to be affected is phenomenal. For the indigenous communities, the scheduled tribes and the scheduled castes, who form two-thirds of the population of the region it is going to be a total disaster. And the project is going to cause the greatest environmental damage ever witnessed by coal mining in the country. The Peiperwar opencast Project is the first step towards this holocaust.

The Project

India's coal reserves are approximately 192.36 bts. as estimated by the Geological Survey of India in 1991, of which 62.08 bts. are found in Chotanagpur and North Karanpur shares 13,578.8 mts. of this. The total reserve of coal at Piparwar is estimated around 244 mts. of which 197 mts. is of power grade coal. The mines will have a life span of 35 years[13] .

The project is being executed under bilateral agreement with the Government of Australia on a turnkey basis which is to be completed in five years. It is reported to be the single largest foreign aided project yet sponsored by the Australian government anywhere. The contract partner is the White Industries Limited of Sydney, Australia. The project was submitted in 1987 by AUSTRADE and the White Industries Ltd. India gave

---

13. Bharat Jan Andolan and Nav Bharat Jagriti Kendra, 1993:4.

approval in 1989, with a final cost of the project estimated to be $500 million (Rs.542 crores). Out of this amount Australian contribution was estimated to be $206.6 million (Rs.244 crores) coming in a mixed credit scheme; $61 million from the Australian International Development Assistance Bureau (AIDAB), and $145m from the Export Finance Insurance Corporation. A condition of the concessional loan package was that the Indian Government use the funds to buy Australian equipments and expertise. Australian manufacturers would sell about $151 m of mining and technical services to the project (approximately 73% of the total equipment). However, the estimated cost has now escalated to Rs.840 crore[14] .

The purpose of the project is to feed two thermal power stations, Dadri in Uttar Pradesh and Yamunanagar in Haryana. Both are World Bank financed projects, and both are of 4 units of 210MWs each. The demand of coal for Dadri will be 2.98 million tonnes, and for Yamunanagar 1.9 million tonnes by 1994-95 .

Geography of the region

North Karanpura valley, longitude 84° - 46° and latitude 23° - 38° on the Tropic of Cancer, is part of a Gondwana strata, a major rift valley dating from the Upper Carboniferous. The extent of the Upper Trough or Basin of North Karanpura is approximately 44 miles in length and 22 miles in width. The valley occupies parts of the districts of Hazaribagh and Chatra; some western part of it lying in Palamau district, while just south of Damodar river at Khalari is the district of Ranchi. The valley is the river valley of the Damodar and flanks of it for the first forty miles of its length through a forested watershed are responsible for the security of the Damodar-Barakar catchment lower down. The Karanpura coalfields were brought to light first by Mr. D.H. Williams

14. ibid

who died there in 1948, and the area was first mapped by Mr. T.W.H. Hughes in 1867.

Structurally, the North Karanpura area consists of three separate basins.

(i) Under the Mahudi hill ranges in the east and along the Satpahari ranges north of McCluskiegunge in Ranchi and Palamau districts.

(ii) The second basin may be described as the Mahilan basin, north-west of McCluskiegunge, and

(iii) The third basin is the Chano or Rikab part-basin which extends from north of Ango eastwards into the Bokaro coalfields. The hill ranges of North Karanpura contains rich forests, teaming wildlife and beautiful flora, several of these indigenous to this region.

People of the region

The valley has been the ancient abode of the Santhals and the Mundas who were later joined by the Uraons, Birhors and the Kurmis. The other communities who settled in later periods are the Karmalis, Bhogtas, Bediyas and Ghatwals. Traditionally, except for the Birhors, all the communities are settled agriculturists. Their economy is partially supplemented by hunting and gathering. Till recent times the region was covered with game-filled forests of the Mahudi hill ranges which run along the Northbanks of Damodar river, along with the Aswa Pahar and Sati ranges forming the basin's Eastern flank, the north escarpments and promontories of the Hazaribagh plateau, jungled ranges of 40 kms. and in the deep western forests outreaching into the adjoining district of Palamau. The Hinduised communities of the region are Chamars, Hajams, Lohars, Kumhars, Telis, Kahars and Baurhees. The opening of the Damodar Valley Project in recent years has brought an increase of outside population which has overpowered the tribal and other indigenous population and their society.

World Heritage Site

The Piparwar Opencast Project is not only alienating the land and the forest traditionally belonging to the tribal and other indigenous peoples of the region but also going to destroy their heritage. The Regional Chapter of the Indian National Trust for Art and Cultural Heritage (INTACH), based in Hazaribagh, has already established the palaeo-archaeological and plao-anthropological character of the region. INTACH is responsible for the discovery of the most significant rock-art site as yet found in the eastern region, as well as continuous stone deposits spanning the time frame from Pleistocene(2m) to the Neolithic (9,000 BC) and down to the Iron Age (1,200 BC) which is a proof of North Karanpura being the cradle of human evolution and birthplace of writing, in expert opinion predating Sumeria by over three thousand years. The remains of atleast two civilisational epochs before the Mauryan empire lie buried under the valley floor littered with traces of the Mesolithic dolmens, Megalithic burial sites, rock-art and cave shelters. As a result of the INTACH's campaign to protect this invaluable "world heritage" the North Karanpura Valley has been declared as a "protected area" by the Ministry of Environment and Forest through gazetted notification along with the Western Ghat, the Arvallis and the Siwaliks.

People's Movement

Piparwar Opencast Coal Mines became operational on the 20th of January, 1989. Immediately the villagers of the area protested against the Central Coalfields Limited's machine drivers and workers commencing any preliminary works, until they were adequately compensated and rehabilitated. For they had bitter experiences of disbursement of compensation by the CCL. The CCL's record on compensation had really been atrocious. For instance, nearby villagers were still awaiting compensation for their farming land taken by the CCL for a mine which closed six years ago. However, six months later, people from several villages held a mass meeting at Bahera and drew up a list of demands. These were principally for compensation for lands and homes, to be settled by the Commissioner of North Chotanagpur; all displaced people to be given jobs; and equivalent land to be allotted for house sites. In 1991, over 2,000 people demonstrated in front of the CCL district offices.

The Year 1992 witnessed a fast growth of the affected people's consolidation and finally the emergence of a popular organisation called "Karanpura Ghati Bachao Jan Andolan". Not only most of the local political parties supported the move but also their members participated in all the meetings held by the organisation. Many concerned individuals and Non-Governmental organisations came out jointly in support of the people's cause. An Action Group was formed on 31st May, 1992 in Hazaribagh to "support the formation of a mass organisation based on democratic principles and committed to the struggle on the main issues of the project affected people". International NGOs also took serious interest in this "anti-people project". In January 1992 a five-member Australian fact-finding team from Community Aid Abroad toured the North Karanpura basins. Carol Sherman, Director Rainforest Information Centre, Australia, visited the Piparwar project in February, 1992. Later on she published a report supporting the people's point of view on the destructive nature of the project. The Public Radio News Service of Australia despatched a report on the project on the 2nd of July, 1992. It condemned the project saying the venture will cause untold damage to the environment and the local people. A team of the Australian Television visited the project in September to cover a mass protest meeting and the plight of the people and their land. The Sun Herald of Australia in its August 9, 1992 issue gave an extensive coverage on the rape of the North Kanapura Basin by the CCL. The project was described as a "Scandal" by the Australian development organisations. A new report by Australian Rainforest Information Centre said, "The local people are being sacrificed for the elite of Indian society and Australian business contracts". "The project is a potential environmental and social disaster", said Jeff

Atkinson, Research Co-ordinator with Community Aid Abroad - the largest Australian Aid Agency, since its merger with Freedom From Hunger Campaign. He said that Indian authorities, judged on their record, could "absolutely not" be trusted to ensure adequate mine rehabilitation and compensation. "AIDAB and White Industries cannot wash their hands off these issues", he said. Penny Lee, Director of Research and Information for the Australian Council for Overseas Aid, said the non-government development sector was united in opposition to the mine. It appears that commercial benefit rather than long-term development has been the incentive for Australia's involvement. The Minewatch, in its Briefing no.19: Piparwar, July, 1992, condemned the Australians as Dirty Diggers". Narrating the extent of destruction caused by the coal mines the Illustrated Weekly of India said, "There are................many areas, some running into hundreds of square kilometers which are unrecognisable after 10 years, especially after CCL has gone through them.......These were once areas of lush forest supporting rich wildlife, or productive paddy fields with their associated villages and tribal hamlets. Now they are unrecognisable as they have been turned into deserts, pits and hillocks of waste soil on which nothing grows[15].

The villages which have been affected or are going to be engulfed by the project very soon are : Magardaha, Benti, Puranadih, Bahera, Kishto, Belari, Kalyanpur, Karo, Rajghar, Sidalu, Bijan, Chora, Basria and a few more neighbouring villages. A leaflet distributed by the Karanpura Ghati Bachao Jan Andolan claimed "this project will make 15 thousand people homeless. Hundreds of acres of forest land will be destroyed. Thousands of farmers will be deprived of their land. The project will jeopardise our traditional culture. It will separate the son from the mother, the brother from the sister, the husband from the wife and the neighbour from the neighbourhood. It will turn us into destitutes".

---

15. Alvarez, Claude and Sarangi, Satinath. "How to Kill a River", Illustrated Weekly of India, August 31st - September 6th, 1991.

The people who will lose their lands, houses, and livelihoods are mainly self-reliant farmers and 41% of them are officially below the poverty line. Although CCL is offering one job for every joint family that has three acres of land or more, this means very little in practice. Many of them affected do not own three acres of land; a joint family may comprise several wage earners, only one of whom may be entitled to employment, and in many cases CCL is cutting down on employment levels. A reduction of over 7,000 workers was set for March, 1992 and a study is underway to sack more workers. Limits have also been placed on overtime and Sunday work, by all CCL subsidiaries. Moreover, it is only "raiyati" or registered land, that CCL considers for compensation. The majority of indigenous peoples were in possession of some land ("gair majurwa") before the registration system was initiated under the British colonial rule. Yet, when people have tried to register this type of land in order to get compensation, the local government refused. Once an order is issued for mining development the people's rights are overridden.

For those who own more than 3 acres of land, some compensation will be paid. However, amounts offered are well below the value of the land. Considering the above mentioned facts the majority of the affected people are gradually subscribing to the call of not to give up their ancestral land for the benefit of a handful of rich and privileged people living in and around Delhi whose ever increasing need for electricity will be met by digging out coal under their land of habitation.

Land Loss

As has already been mentioned the total mining activities in the North Karanpura valley under the CCL, according to the present estimate, will cover 1,230 square kilometers. With 23 more mines to follow shortly Piparwar Opencast Project stands as a first in the area covering at the moment an area of 6.38 sq.kms[16]. If we are to take the averages of people affected in the already existing mines, the displacement caused by them in the next decades will be of alarming proportions. It is compounded by three other factors :

(a) Firstly, it is being done in a comparatively compact geographical area

(b) Secondly, it is being carried out on a very fast time-schedule, and thirdly,

(c) the majority of the people to be affected are scheduled tribes and castes, the ones least capable of coping with such displacement. The predicted social disruption will be of enormous magnitude[17]

The following table gives us the details of the villages losing land to the Piparwar Project.

Villages	Area (Ha)	Area Acquired	%SC & ST Population
Mahgardaha	241.31	247.35	38.67
Kishto	688.02	188.35	41.15
Benti	1133.25	472.48	82.79
Bahera	193.91	153.45	27.32
Bijain	251.35	222.33	92.56
Kanauda	94.97	58.66	00.00
Rajghar	103.83	07.44	49.48

16. Carol Sherman, "The Peoples' Story, AID/CD, 1993

17. B.J.A. & N.B.J.K. 1993. op. cit. pp.5-6

Kalyanpur	757.15	48.41	86.55
Karp	759.94	80.36	62.55
Total	**4223.55**	**1478.8364.11**	

(Source : ibid,p.14)

In 1958 India became signatory to the International Labour Organisation's Convention No.107 by which it agreed that indigenous or tribal oustee families "be provided with land of quality at least equal to that of the lands previously occupied by them, suitable to provide for present needs and future development". However, in contravention to that agreement, in the case of Piparwar, land for land is not being given as compensation.

Case Study - 4 :

Netarhat Field Firing Range

The latest onslaught on the society of the indigenous peoples of Jharkhand is now in the offing in the form of the Netarhat Field Firing Ranges which is going to obliterate 245 villages at a time from the tribal map of the country and leaving approximately 2,24,940 people landless and homeless. Now no clarion call for "national development" is being heard. What is evident is the roaring gums declaring the "operation genocide" of the Adivasis. This time it is more direct and cruel, devastating and far reaching in its impact on the people which they are absolutely incapable of withstanding. Now the slogan is "national interest" for which the biggest displacement and largest land loss of the Adivasis are going to take place at one single blow in Gumla and Palamau districts of Chotanagpur. Now it is not the "capital" but the "cartridge" which is going to dictate the terms. For Field Firing and Artillery Practices of the 23rd Artillery Brigade the Indian Army is going to occupy the ancestral land of the indigenous peoples where not a soul without the uniform would be allowed to move.

The people

The area of the two districts of Palamau and Gumla which is being planned to be brought under army occupation at present was the first entry point of the early Kerowars[18] in Jharkhand. Later on they were joined by the Uraons and in a much later period the Cheros migrated to the region. Except for the Saranda in the district of West Singhbhum this is the only area where the trace of the ancient forest is still visible. In this area, therefore, the concentration of the tribal population is much higher than the other parts of the two districts. The descendants of the early settlers such as the Mundas, Birhors, Korwas, Asurs (Austro-Asaitic language speaking) have still been able to retain some ancestral land in the face of continuous aggression. The Aurs, Birhors, Korwas and the Birjias are, however, considered to be on the verge of extinction by the Governmnt. The area has the last remnants of the Asur tribe, the descendants of the ancient iron smelters of India. Fewer than 8,000 of them live today and all of them are in this area. The same is the case with the Birjias, only a scanty population of about 5,000 of them survives now. About 95% of the kisans live in this area. So also most of the 19,000 Korwas. All of them are hunter-gatherers who largely depend on forest for their livelihood. If the project is implemented they will disappear from the tribal map of India for ever.

Background

The Army has been using the Netarhat Plateau for their Field Firing practices since 1956. In 1981-82 the Army made an attempt to acquire the land covering the area under Netarhat, ChorMunda, Dumberpat, Naina, Arahans, Harmadaulatoli, Husmu and Pakripat. But owing to the opposition from the people and local

---

18. The ancestors of the Austro-Asiatic language speaking Mundas, Santhals, Hos, Korwas and present day Kherowars.

politicians they kept the plan of acquisition in abeyance. Around September, 1992 the Army used the State and the Central Government and succeeded in getting the Governor of Bihar to issue Gazette Notifications to authorise Field Firing practices in the area, in exercise of the powers conferred by sub-section (I) of Section 9 of Maneuvers Field Firing and Artillery Practices Act, 1938 (Act V of 1938).

The first set of notifications issued on November 25, 1991 (Nos.S.O.761 and 762) referred to 66 villages in Gumla and 23 villages in Palamau districts. The second set of notifications issued on March 24 and 28, 1992 (Nos. S.O. 84 & 85) referred to another 127 villages in Gumla and 19 in Palamau, taking the total number of affected villages to 245. (see the table).

It has now been revealed that initially in response to a request from the Army, the State Government had identified a large plot of land near the Deori Dumri Village in Gaya district. What irks the tribals of Palamau and Gumla districts is the lame excuse given by the government later on for the shifting of the firing range from Gaya to the above districts. The Government's excuse is that Deori Dumri has several historical monuments nearby, besides having dense population. This excuse exposes the "blatant ethnocentrism" on the part of the decision makers of the country. Tribal people and their history and heritage do not touch their sensitivity even remotely, particularly when the interests of the tribal and the non-tribal clash. The anti-tribal attitude of the government is further revealed in the statement made by Brigadier I.J. Kumar in a press conference held at Ranchi on 10.12.1993. "The 23rd Infantry Division, infact, co-operated with the state government in turning down the initial proposal (obviously made by the Army) of acquisition of land at Deori Dumri......Subsequently, a large chunk of land near Netarhat was identified for the purpose by the State Government........We have demanded only 188 sq. kms. of area in a sparsely populated area. The State Government, however, earmarked an area 6 times larger than our proposal. (The Hindustan Times).

Loss of land and life

The recent notified area for the firing range is 1471 sq.kms. of which the Government wants to acquire immediately 188 sq.kms. for the impact area and 9 sq.kms. at Adar (Bishunpur Block) and 9 sq.kms. in Netarhat (Mahuadan Block) for Army Camps, totaling 206 sq.kms. This seems to be only the tip of an iceberg as can be seen in the report of Hindustan Times, Patna 14.1.1994, which says that the State Government has proposed 1 lac sq.kms. in Palamau and Gumla districts for the firing range out of which 19,856 sq.kms. will be used as the impact area. This gives credence to the fact since in the earlier notifications around 1956 the government notified only 308 sq.kms. which in 1992 increased to 1471 sq.kms. (vide Notification No.S.O. 761 dated 25.11.91 and Notification No.S.O. 84 dated 28.3.1992). As per these Notifications under Maneuvers, Field Firing and Artillery Practice Act, 1938, the Army will have full control of the area from 12th May, 1992 to 11th May, 2002. This firing range as it stands today will affect more than 2,50,000 people living in more than 245 villages. On the spot field study of the project-map reveals that the inhabitants of around 40 villages of adjoining districts of Surguja in Madhya Pradesh are also going to be displaced by the same project. They are mostly Adivasis. The following table gives us the details of the villages to be occupied.

Block	*District*	*No. of Villages*	*Notification 1991*	*Year 1992*	*Total*
Mahuadanr	Palamau	52	23	29	52
Bishunpur	Gumla	70	38	32	70
Chainpur	Gumla	46	24	22	46
Dumri	Gumla	30	00	30	30
Ghagra	Gumla	42	04	38	42
Gumla	Gumla	05	00	05	05
Total	**6**	**2 245**	**89 +**	**156**	**245**

The project will not only disrupt human life by depriving people of their rights on land and forest but devastate the Betla National Park, its abundant wildlife and bio-diversity. The nearby Project Tiger Reserve is also expected to be affected by pollution from the heavy mortar firing.

People's Response, Organisation and Agitation

Despite the periodic camping, test and survey by the Army every year since 1956, people of the area had never suspected any foul play. It was around September 1992, when strong rumours about the proposed Army camp started to spread around. The people, however, mistakenly thought that the camp would be confined to Netarhat and its adjoining villages where test firing usually had been carried out during the past years.

Around July 1993, some people including the local leaders grew suspicious of a much greater plan, because they noticed more frequent movements of the Army vehicles into the area and also the aerial survey by Army planes and helicopters. Some people discreetly inquired from the Army officials what was going on. The latter showed the acquisition map and related documents to the farmers. The Army personnel had told the people to maintain silence about the issue. But the lid was off by 20.9.1993, as survey and verification procedures were now in full swing in Netarhat and adjoining areas. The people had discovered to their horror that the rumour of land acquisition by the Army had indeed become a stark reality.

Without losing time, local leaders sounded alarm in the area and began to search for capable leaders from among themselves for mobilising the people against the impending displacement. Thy held a meeeting on 25.9.1993 and decided to oppose the displacement move of the Army by forming Jan Sangharsh Samitis in the entire affected areas of Palamau and Gumla Districts. It was further decided that the nature of the Samitis would be non-political, non-religious, non-denominational and without any caste basis. Expenses would be met from the contribution of the affected people themselves. Call for unity was greatly emphasised. The Pramukh, Mukhiyas, Sarpanches and Panches at Panchayat level were immediately entrusted with the leadership in opposing the project.

The Pramukh of Mahuadanr sent notices on 26.9.1993 to all Panchayats for the first public meeting on the subject. Copies of the notice were also served for information to the Block, Anchal and Thana. Through this meeting the public registered protest against the proposed land acquisition and decided to send memoranda to the President of India, the Prime Minister, the Governor of Bihar, the Chief Minister and other ministers of the State and Central levels. Prior to the meeting, every village had elected 5 representatives who were to coordinate the village level Sangharsh Samitis. All these representatives met on 27.9.1993 to elect the Jan Sangharsh Samiti, Chhechhari, that would coordinate and represent their interests in public fora. The dedication of local leaders, sound advice of well wishers and generous cooperation of the public of Chhechhari helped the mobilisation drive go faster. The meeting held on 27.9.1993 was attended by about 10,000 people from all corners of the valley. After the meeting, a memorandum addressed to the President of India was handed over to the C.O. of Mahuadanr.

As per the decision of the meeting on 27.9.1993, about 5000 people staged a demonstration in front of the D.C. and Commissioner's office at Daltonganj. The said officials were absent on the day. More petitions were being sent opposing the Project to various Government Ministries, both at the State and Central Levels.

The Jan Sangharsh Samiti is closely monitoring the movement against the land acquisition by the Army. It is on guard against the elements with vested and political interests. Its upper most concern is the protection of the people's rights and the problems of displacement. Non-political forces, including the local intelligentsia and other similar organisations are to help the Sangharsh Samitis sharpen their focus on the central issue.

The Palamau Students Union had organised an anti-Project demonstration in Ranchi on 13.10.1993. It acted as a trial blazer for the youth of Barway and Banari-Bishunpur areas who organised themselves to join with the Palamau students wing.

A massive rally was held by the Jan Sangharsh Samiti on 17.10.1993 at Mahuadanr. In this meeting a sizeable number of people from Barway had also taken part. They in turn carried the torch of mass awakening to Barway area. The meeting was covered by four new reporters from Daltonganj and one reporter each from Delhi and Ranchi.

Sri Shyam Narayan Dubey, the BJP leader and Vice-President of the Vananchal Pradesh Samiti, is the only person in the entire Palamau and Gumla Districts to have supported the Project in the name of "national interest (The Nav Bharat Times, October 6, 1993). As it is clear Sri Dubey is a non-tribal and therefore, it is not surprising that he has no sympathy for the tribal cause in question. In this regard, other BJP leaders of the area too have been conspicuous by their tight-lipped silnce and apathy. This was of course expected.

On 28.10.1993, Sri Shiv Prasad Sahu, erstwhile MLA (Cong.I), had reportedly held a public meeting at Bishunpur and Adar to announce that the Government had no proposal to establish Army camps in Gumla District. In order to prove his credibility he distributed in large numbers photo copies of supposedly authentic letter No.30 PM 93 - Defence (Q&C), dated 8.9.1993, of Sri V.P. Raja, Joint Secretary of the Central Defence Ministry. Similar announcements were made by other Congress members at various places in the affected area. In addition, the press (The Aaj, October 29, 1993; and the Hindustan Times, October 30, 1993) also speeded up the wide publicity of the above announcement. The impact on the people of such announcements was misleading and confusing. The protest movement which was gathering momentum suffered a serious set back for some-time. There was a momentary lull in the air and silence had enveloped the people.

Some informed individuals, however, kept on investigating into the matter. Fortunately, in the course of investigation the above mentioned gazette Notifications were discovered. As a result, the movement received a shot in the arm. The informations contained in the above documents, however, could not be speedily sent out to remote villages. Hence, fresh waves of awakening programmes were planned.

On 25.11.1993, Palamau Students' Union and Hira Barway Students' Union had a joint meeting in Ranchi. They decided to revive the protest movement by giving correct informations to the public. They promptly dispersed into different corners of the affected areas with the copies of the two Gazette Notifications mentioned above. Besides many village level meetings, there were 3 successive public meetings held at Loadih, Rajawal and Katkahi on 5th. 7th and 12th December, 1993. Similarly meetings were held in Mahuadanr area too. Importantly, the Central Jan Sangharsh Samiti inaugurated its office in Chomunda on December 8, 1993, to keep up the fight against the above Field Firing Range Project. The office is to monitor every new development regarding the said Project. On December 19, 1993, students in Ranchi observed Human Rights Day. Many of them had returned from an intensive field exposure in the affected areas of the Project. Various awareness programmes were conducted to which many youth groups of Ranchi had been invited.

There was yet another meeting of the above mentioned two Students' Unions held on 16.12.1993 in Ranchi. Significantly, the newly formed Banari-Bishunpur Students' Union also joined this meeting. On that occasion, the three Students Organisations decided to work together. They chalked out programmes to be carried out in the villages. As part of their programme, a delegation of students met the Divisional Commissioner of Chotanagpur on 21.12.1993. They decided to submit a memorandum to Sri Rajesh Pilot, Union Home Minister of State, on 8.1.1994. It had been announced that he was going to visit Ranchi. It was learnt later that probably having sensed the ground-swell of the protest movement, Rajesh Pilot cancelled his announced visit to Ranchi.

The 23rd Artillery Brigade had completed all preparations for Field Firing in one dozen villags to take place on 23rd and 24th March, 1994. The Central Jan Sangharsh Samiti passed on the message to all the people through nagara (drum) in every village that a memorandum would be sent to the concerned Army Authorities, appealing to them not to carry out the field firing. If they did not reply by 22nd March, villagers would take out a victory procession with the demand for withdrawal of field firing. However, the villagers took control of the roads from Jokipokhar to Adar and Netarhat from 20th March onwards by coming on the roads with massive blockades on them. The Army personnel with their military vehicles were told to go back on 23d March and they, in fact, began to retreat (The Jansatta, March 24, 1994).

In a unique display of solidarity, on April 9, 1994 more than ten thousand Adivasis marched through the streets of Delhi in protest against the forceful acquisition of 230 thousand hectares of forest and agricultural land in Chotanagpur. According to Chhawni Visthapan Sangharsh Samiti, Palamau, approximately 2,24,940 people are to be displaced from the Blocks of Mahuadanr, Chainpur, Dumri, Ghagra and Gumla in the Gumla districts of South Bihar.

The Delhi rally, organised by Adivasi Yuva Samiti of Delhi, was attended by Adivasis from Chotanagpur now residing in Delhi. The protesters and supporters raised slogans like "*Jaan denge, par jameen nahin denge*" and "*Jan jan ka nara hai, zamin jangal hamara hai*". They beat traditional drums and pledged to protect land, forest and water even sacrificing their lives.

Meanwhile on the same day more than 10,000 Netarhat Field Firing Range Project affected Tribals flocked to Ranchi to protest against the large scale displacement in the name of Nation's Security. More than 50,000 Adivasis were blocking the roads at Jokipokhar - Tutwapani.

The Ranchi rally which started off from Sainik Bazaar and culminated in a Public Meeting at Bari Park was organised under the banner of "**Netarhat Field Firing Range Project Sangharsh Samiti**". This organisation was formed recently, amalgamating several tribal organisations working for the same cause including Chhawni Visthapan Sangharsh Samiti, Palamau, the Heera-Barwe Students' Association and the Palamau Students' Association. Dominic Tirkey is the President and Mukund Ram the Secretary of the new organisation.

Besides others, Dr. B.D. Sharma, former Commissioner, Scheduled Tribes and Scheduled Castes, Bandi Oraon, Vice-Chairman State SC&ST Commission and Karma Oraon, BPSC Vice-Chairman spoke at the public meeting. The gathering demanded in unison the immediate revocation of the Bihar Gazette Notifications that authorized, in a specified area "*the carrying out periodically of Field Firing and Artillery Practices for a period of ten years commencing from 12th May, 1992 and ending with May 2002*".

Case study : 5**

RORO IRRIGATION PROJECT : WEST SINGHBHUM

Given the fact that 70% of the Indian population is involved in agriculture related production, the development of agricultural production has been a point

** The paper is based upon personal experience and literature prepared by the support groups and the affected people themselves.

of concern of the Indian planners especially after the launching of the Five-Year Plans. The Third Five-Year Plan particularly aimed at starting a process of development both at the level of the agricultural infrastructure as well as the more modern methods of agricultural production. Part of the development of agricultural infrastructure is land and water development. It consisted of major, medium and minor irrigation projects. While the major and medium irrigation projects were composed of large and medium-sized dams, reservoirs etc., the minor irrigation schemes were mainly directed towards exploiting the irrigation potential through canals, tanks, irrigation wells and tube wells.

Although the need and relevance of irrigation development through canals etc. are valid, the manner in which the Bihar government went about implementing it in Bihar was doomed to failure from the very start. The south-Bihar plateau has tremendous potential for minor irrigation development, given the mountain terrain and the numerous rivers and rivulets.

But the minor irrigation projects were ill conceived, technically faulty, administratively inefficient and financially corrupt. Consequently, of the numerous irrigation projects that were started all over the Jharkhand region during the last three decades, many have been given up half way; others remain dysfunctional even if physically completed. The only thing that has definitely happened is that the small farmers, majority of whom are tribals, have lost part or whole of their land for good without a share in the benefits in terms of better irrigation facilities. When the people are deprived of their land under the guise of promises of irrigation facilities, and when years pass without the promised irrigation available to them, it really is a situation of violation of their human rights.

1. THE PROJECT

A research-study was undertaken by the Jharkhandis' Organisation for Human Rights (JOHAR) of

Singhbhum under the guidance of Mr. Stan Lurdswamy, on the Roro Canal Irrigation Project during the summer of 1994. The field-study was done by a group of ten students who were themselves Jharkhandis. The purpose of the study was to highlight the extent of land alienation of the Jharkhandi people, majority of whom are indigenous tribal people, under the pretension of providing irrigation schemes in the Jharkhand region, the great majority of which are either incomplete or even if complete are dysfunctional. JOHAR-SINGHBHUM chose this Roro Canal Irrigation Project in west Singhbum as a sample to scientifically establish the fact that the real purpose on the part of the Indian government is not the development of the indigenous people but further impoverishment through a systematic process of land alienation. The name of the game is "local development". The study addresses itself to supporting people's movements. The style in which the report is written is from the people's point of view; as such it is "partisan" and "pro-people". Hence in the present form it may be viewed as "subjective" in the executive and judiciary circles. This is a conscious, deliberate choice on the part of those involved in doing and reporting the study. Right now it is meant to enlighten, educate and raise the consciousness level of the people who are the victims of the "development process" carried on by the government. It is hoped that depending on the type of action the people will decide to undertake, more documentary evidence can be incorporated into the report that will give it the colour of "objectivity" and "legal validity".

(a) *Some facts about the project:*

According to the *District Statistical Hand Book of the Government of Bihar for 1973-74* Roro Irrigation Project was completed in 1970. The total investment into the project was Rs.134 lakhs. As per the estimate of the government, the potential of irrigation through the canal is 22,400 acres during the Kharif (monsoon) season and 4,600 acres during the Rabi (winter) season; of this, in the year 1973-74 the government discovered that the actually irrigated land was 8,523 acres during the Kharif and 98.80

acres during the Rabi season[19]. Even this figure is highly disputable as will be shown in the analysis of the survey. The acquisition of land for the purpose of the canal was done during 1961-65.

(b) *The area and methodology of study :*

The Roro Canal runs from Chaibasa in a north direction and is approximately 25 kms. long; the study was done in 37 villages of three Blocks:

4	villages of Chaibasa Block
23	in Khuntpanil and
10	in Sareikela

All in all, *377 households* whose land was acquired for the canal were studied:

72	household in Chaibasa Block
286	in Khuntpani and
19	in Sareikela

The way the householders were approached was through the traditional (Munda/Manki) leadership of the tribal community: on the day previously agreed with the leaders, the researchers met the members of all the households of the village in the presence of the leaders when the objectives of the study was explained to them, and the members of each household who had given land for the canal were interviewed in their own respective homes.

A questionnaire was used as guide to elicit response from the people. It was also clearly communicated to the concerned people that once the

---

19. District Statistics, 1973-74, p.276

whole study was done, the findings will be personally communicated to them and that it will be they who, as the affected people, will decide on the course of action to be taken.

(c) *Some limitations :*

One main difficulty experienced by the researchers was the fact that the Roro Canal Project was implemented 30 years ago, several of those who were actually forced to surrender their land for the project were dead and gone. Their children who are now grown up adults are not in the know of precise information such as the exact amount of land, the total compensation amount the family received, etc. An effort was made to overcome this limitation by spending more time with older men who were still around.

Another limitation was getting to see documents related to land acquisition and vouchers and receipt for payment of land and water-tax. Most households have lost the documents, if at all they were given any; however, several households were able to show the receipts.

The reader will notice that the total number of responses for the different queries of the questionnaire do not always equal to 377; sometimes it will be more and at other times it will be less. The reason for this variation is the fact that when the members of a household were interviewed, more than one adult members came forward with their response, and in other cases of elderly persons were not there and the younger adult members were not in the know of things and as such could not furnish an answer.

(d) *Population covered :*

In terms of *Community classification,* of the 377 households covered,

362 (96%) belong to Scheduled Tribes,

14 (4%) belongs to Scheduled castes and one single household to Other Backward Classes (OBC).

As such, the overwhelming majority are the indigenous tribal people. As for *family size.*

60 households are small (less than 5 members)

81 are medium (5-8 members) and

280 are large (more than 8 members).

It is noted, especially in the case of large households, that they are not nuclear families with husband, wife and children; rather, they are a kind of joint-families with grown up children, some of them may be married and, therefore, with their spouses and children and others still to be settled. Often even the hearth may be more than one, but the family members live in the different portions of a large house sharing a common yard ("angan"), with the older parents still with them, and family property not yet divided. Strictly speaking, according to census norms, every hearth should mean one family. In the case of tribal communities in the Jharkhand region, and therefore in this present case, one has to take a more flexible view in understanding family-size.

(e) *The age-grouping of the population consists of*

1437 (44%) children

1307 (40%) adults and

485 (16%) old people.

Given the nature of the study where we have to go 30 years back in history, the older generation is the better equipped part of the population to give the needed information with regard to land-acquisition; yet, this older generation is also largely illiterate and, therefore, unable to give precise figures in terms of acreage of land owned and land given for the purpose of the canal, nor have they been able to preserve the documents and receipts. Despite these limitations, the researchers, appreciated the very valid information obtained from them.

(f) *The occupation of the heads of household :*

348 (81%) are directly involved in agriculture-related activities

82 (19%) are employed outside either on a full or part-time basis.

It means that the great majority of the people affected by the canal are dependent on agriculture for their sustenance. Agriculture means land, and land means the wherewithal for survival as small farmers. Keeping in mind the fact that the tribal people in Jharkhand region mostly belong to the small-farmer category and the method of cultivation continues to be by and large traditional, land is vital for their existence. This vital factor is precisely what is being attacked by the outside forces and particularly by the government.

II. THE LAND ACQUISITION PROCESS :

(a) *The decision about the project :*

As elsewhere, the government of Bihar decided on implementing the Roro Canal Project without any reference to the people concerned. The people of these 37 villages were neither consulted nor was their consent sought. The local government did not even take the trouble to call village meetings to explain the proposed project to the people. In fact, if the government had sought the views of the people, they with their own insights in water management, would have advised against the project or at least suggested some crucial modifications to the project for its effective functioning. None of this was done.

On the contrary, the authorities of the Minor Irrigation Department of the Government of Bihar summoned the tribal leaders in groups and informed them about the commencement of the project for which acquisition of land was the first step. The leaders were told to cooperate with the government so that the land acquisition could take place without any problem. This was in 1961. Notifications were served to the concerned households in terms of Survey Number, Plot Number, acres and decimals. All these technical jargons did not mean anything to the mostly illiterate people who were used to an entirely different set of measurements such as "bighas", and even these bighas were of different sizes in different areas. So, exactly how much and which portion of their land was being acquired by the government was a mystery to the people until they saw the canals being dug and embankments being constructed. If the household had some knowledgeable persons who could argue with the supervisors and workmen, it would be possible to ensure that only the notified size of the land was taken over from them; if, on the other hand, the head of household was poor, illiterate and afraid of facing government people and as such could not speak for himself, more land than what was notified was liberally taken over. The same dynamics operated when it came to compensation that would be paid for the land.

When the researchers asked to see the documents, only 15% of the respondents were able to produce them. 31% said they never had them and 54% said they had them at one time but lost them eventually. And even these so-called "documents" consisted mostly of receipts and vouchers for land-tax and water tax, and very few documents relating to the land acquisition and compensation.

(b) *The process of canal construction :*

With regard to the proximity of the canal to the physical location of the house holds.

285 (75%) households are within 1 km distance

73 (19%) between 1 to 2 km and

19 (6%) more than 2 kms from the canal.

This means that most of the people who gave their land for the purpose of the canal are practically looking at the canal everyday and realising that they have not drawn any benefit from the canal in terms of better irrigation facilities. And yet, development of irrigation was the precise purpose announced by the government.

(c) *The amount of land taken over from the people for the canal construction out of a total 358 households:*

171 (48%) have given land up to one acre,

126 (35%) between one to two acres and

61 (17%) more than two acres.

The members of 19 households had no response whatever because on the one hand there are no elderly persons living any more, and on the other hand they do not have any documents in their possession. All they know is that their foreparents had given some land for the canal.

The above situation makes it very difficult to arrive at an exact estimation of the land taken over by the government. A very rough estimate as a possible minimum would be :

171 x 1 = 171

126 x 2 = 252

61 x 3 = 183

Total = 606 acres

The point of concern is also the use to which it was put. More light on this will be thrown later in the study when the proclaimed purpose of the canal, the compensation paid to the people and the actual use of the canal are discussed.

(d) *The government's stated objectives for the canal, leading to the acquisition of land from the people, was understood as follows :*

Out of the 436 responses elicited on this point,
379 (87%) persons perceived it as irrigation development,

45 (10%) perceived it rather vaguely as local development and remaining 12 persons (3%) could not recall anything specific.

There can be no doubt about "development of irrigation" being the main objective because this project is officially listed in the Minor Irrigation Schemes in the District Statistical Hand Book of the Bihar Government. What happened to this irrigation objective is something yet to be examined from the rest of the study.

(e) *The role of local leaders*

As the local government started to acquire people's land and commence work on canal construction, what was the role of the local leaders in reference to the people?

Out of the 124 mostly older persons,

101 (81%) recalled that the traditional (Munda/Manki) leadership went along with the government, and did nothing to help the people even to raise questions, seek clarifications and extract clear assurances from the government.

18(15%) felt that the government-associated (Mukhia/Sarpanch) personalities played a key role in persuading people to surrender their land, and a small group of 5 persons (4%) felt that the local MLA was also roped in by the government to tell the people that they better go along with the government's plan.

A people who know for sure that land is the only source of survival would naturally be hesitant to part with their land. But for them to act, they would need leaders who would lead and guide them. This was what the people needed most, but they did not have it.

And how come the traditional tribal leadership just went along with the government? We need to recall the historical process introduced by the Indian Government since independence, of systematically sidelining the tribal social system of which their leadership is an integral part. By imposing the Panchayat System on the tribal people the government succeeded in marginalising the traditional leadership and robbing it of its authority, self-respect, dignity and substituted it with the syndrome of Mukhia/Sarpanch of the Panchayati Raj. They are the elected leaders at the Panchayat-level and sometimes one finds non-tribals living in nearby town-markets getting themselves or their hand-picked tribals elected to the post with their money power and boss over the villages coming under their jurisdiction. The traditional tribal leadership has now been pretty much reduced to be an innocuous entity and is often made use of by the government-bureaucrats as pawns to manipulate the people. Worst of all is the fact that the Mundas have been made the official tax-collectors to the government, collecting land and water taxes from the people, thus becoming "government-agents". No wonder, then, in the present case the traditional tribal leadership did not rise up to the occasion to safeguard the interests of the people, but instead persuaded them to hand over their land to the government.

(f) *The people, therefore, could not muster any resistance to the project. Of the 350 responses to this query,*

194 (55%)	said there was no resistance at all,
64 (18%)	said that a few individuals protested to the government authorities about the improprieties committed by the government servants and petty officials in the process of land acquisition, and

87 (25%) confided that at least in some villages people put-up some resistance collectively although it could not be sustained for long given the ruthlessness of the government officials and the lack of support from their own leaders.

One of the manifestations of the government's ruthlessness was attested to by 172 persons; of them,

132 (77%) testified that after the notifications were issued, people were restricted from ploughing their land, and

17(10%) recalled that rural credit-loans were stopped by the government.

(g) *Pressure on the people*

All this indicates the fact that the government exerted pressure on the people to accept the canal project. Out of the 273 responses on this point,

251 (92%) felt that the government had decided on the project and nothing that the people did could stop it; in other words, there was no way out for the people except to accept it.

So the next best thing was to go along with it and give their land and hope for the best; 385 persons responded as follows :

106 (28%) said they believed in the government's promise of providing better irrigation.

79 (21%) felt assured of getting at least some benefit,

62 (16%) were afraid of denying the government, and

137 (37%) felt helpless in the situation.

The end result was that the people were forced to part with their land and reconcile themselves to the fact of the canal coming in their midst with the uncertain hope that at least some benefit will accrue to them.

(h) *The role of government officials*

In this process of giving their land for the canal project, running to the government offices to get the compensation money, putting forward certain requests for the consideration of government officials such as not to acquire certain common places like land for worship ("Sarna") etc., the people got an inkling of the attitude and disposition of the mostly non-tribal outsider government officials towards them. Of the 353 persons who responded to the query about the role of the government officials.

340 (96%)	felt the government officials were not only unhelpful but also indifferent and sometimes even arrogant in their dealings with the people, and only
13(14%)	said they found the government officials helpful.

III. THE PROCESS OF COMPENSATION

This was a process of injustice perpetrated against the people. If the arbitrary taking over of land for an ill-conceived, technically flawed project was unfair, it was even more so when it came to compensating the people for their land.

(a) First of all, the criteria of *fixing the rate of compensation* was set by the government all on its own without any reference to the people concerned. Of the 403 persons who expressed their opinion on this, 387 (96%) testified that the government alone fixed it and people were kept in the dark. What is more, the casual way in which the compensation money was disbursed is even more disturbing. The people were also issued official notifications, one for the acquisition of their land and another for getting the compensation. The irony was that these notifications were in many cases in English and in other cases in Hindi. The government communicating in English to rural tribal population which during the 1960s was more than 80% illiterate, was the height of nonsense. Such an action on the part of the government clearly brings out the fact that it could not care less whether the people concerned understood the official communication or not; all that mattered was that a semblance of legal procedure was adhered to and that people's land was acquired for the project.

And when the people did go to the land acquisition office, they were made to go time and again before finally getting the compensation money the government designed to give them. Of course, the ordeal of running around to get the money could be shortened if the Project Officer's palms were greased. Out of the 66 persons who ventured to state this fact, 31 (47%) said they had to bribe the project officers in order to get their money released soon.

Was the compensation fair? From among the 374 persons who reflected on this.

296 (79%) said it was below the market value and that the people were cheated,

47 (13%) felt that the more poor and illiterate among them were cheated even more, sometimes as little as Rs.200/- for an acre of land, and

only 23 (6%) said they received as per the market value.

This brings out a situation of wholesale corruption on the part of the government functionaries in disbursing the compensation money to the people. The more the people are economically and socially weak, the greater the chances of being made the victims of corruption.

What was the rate per acre of land that was followed as the norm for compensation? Was it on par with the then market rate? These are the questions that the local Land Acquisition Office refuses to answer despite repeated efforts to get them.

(b) Now, coming to the *actual compensation money received by the people*, the following details were obtained. Only 155 households out of the total 377 were able to furnish this information because only these had some older members who actually surrendered their land for the project.

65 (42%) received between Rs. 1 to 500

41 (26%) received between Rs. 501 to 1000

32 (21%) received between Rs. 1001 to 2000

11 (07%) received between Rs. 2001 to 5000

04 (02%) received between Rs. 50001 to 10,000

02 (01%) received between Rs. 10,001 to 20,000

It would not serve any purpose in trying to estimate the total money received by the people because it will be much too inflated if we take the outer maximum margin and too short if we take the inner minimum margin. One important thing to take note of is that the great majority (89%) of the people received less than Rs.2000, a significant majority (68%) received less than Rs.1000, and a little less than half (42%) the population received less than Rs.500 as compensation for their land. This was no great deal for the people.

However, a serious anomaly comes to light when we consider the fact that 48% of the people had given up to one acre of their land (see previous table on amount of land), and that means the real of compensation for one acre of land was around Rs.500. This is confirmed by the fact that another 35% of them had given between 1 to 2 acres of their land, and they got a compensation of upto

Rs.1000. Even though it was 30 years ago, Rs.500 per acre of good agricultural land seems a pittance indeed.

Here also, our efforts to get the total amount of compensation disbursed by the local government proved futile.

(c) The *utilisation of he compensation money* by the people is quite revealing. Out of the 406 responses to this query.

15 (4%)	used if for land purchase,
12 (3%)	used it for land development,
43 (11%)	used it for house construction,
188 (46%)	used if for purchase of household articles,
90 (22%)	used it for cattle, and
58 (14%)	used it for consumer items.

So only a tiny little 7% population was to invest the money on land proper; 4% on purchase of land and 3% on development of their land. As for the great majority, land which is their permanent asset was made to melt away into less permanent, usufructory purposes. Whole or part of their land is gone for good.

After having gone through the whole process of land acquisition, compensation and the use of the compensation money, how did the people feel about the whole process? Of the 373 persons who expressed their feelings about this.

344 (92%)	said they were very dissatisfied, and felt cheated by the government, and
only 29(8%)	said they were satisfied with what they got from the government and the use they made of it.

If an overwhelming 92% of the people are very unhappy about the whole process and even feel cheated, there is enough ground for it. After sacrificing their land for more and better irrigation as per the word of the government, if they had seen it happening, then the dissatisfaction would most certainly be less. But what they have experienced during the past 30 years was not more irrigation but less irrigation. During all these years, very little water has flowed in the canal for irrigational purposes. More details about this fact in the ensuing part.

IV. THE PRESENT REALITY IN TERMS OF IRRIGATION

(a) Actual Benefit

The land of the people was acquired and canal was dug for the explicitly stated purpose of providing irrigation facilities to the farmers of these 37 villages. And three decades have passed since. How much have the farmers benefited in terms of irrigation? The 349 persons who responded to this question testified as follows -

291 (83%)	said they have not benefited at all from the canal,
23 (07%)	said they irrigated upto one acre from the canal water,
29 (08%)	said they irrigated between 2 to 5 acres, and
6 (02%)	said they irrigated between 6 to 10 acres.

In terms of acreage, it will roughly add up to;

23 x 01 = 23
29 x 05 = 145
06 x 10 = 60
Total = 228 acres irrigated from the canal water.

Even taking the liberal outer margin of 228 acres, it compares very unfavourably with the figures officially projected by the government, viz. 8,523 acres during the Kharif crop period and 98.80 acres during the Rabi crop period. This is further complicated by yet another official assessment done by the Waterway Department in 1993 where the irrigation-potential of Roro Irrigation Canal is stated to be 5,500 hectares (=13,750 acres).

(b) When queried about the *duration of irrigation* through the course of the year, 371 persons answered as follows :

185 (50%)	said there is no flowing water sufficient to irrigate their land during any part of the year.
175 (47%)	said only during monsoon season there is flowing water in the canal, and
11 (03%)	said there is water available round the year.

The first category of persons testifying that there is no water at all in the canal sufficient for irrigation purposes mostly belong to the villages which are 10 kms. and more from Chaibasa. One can see only puddles of water and that too only during monsoon, and that is not the water for irrigation.

The second category of persons are from villages closer to Chaibasa and as such there is some water in the canal during monsoon, but they rarely use the water for irrigation . Besides, if the monsoon is good, there would be no need for the canal water.

The third very small category of persons who say there is water in the canal right round the year are those who live in the immediate vicinity of Chaibasa and who are also better equipped with pumpsets etc.

(c) On being asked as to which are the *crops grown with canal water*, of the 352 responses,

322 (91%)	testified that they grow no crop at all with the canal water, and
27 (08%)	said that they grow one monsoon crop with the help of canal water insofar as they supplement canal water when the monsoon is irregular or fails.

Obviously then, the canal is not of any benefit to most farmers in their agriculture; yet the canal project was implemented precisely to provide irrigation to farmers.

(d) If the canal is not serving the purpose of irrigation, is it *used for any other purpose* at all by the people living along side the canal? Out of the 470 persons offering a response,

228 (49%)	do not use the canal water at all for any purpose because water is never there,
64 (14%)	use it for bathing,
90 (19%)	use it for washing and
77(16%)	use it for their cattle.

The question is whether the canal was constructed for these other purposes, and whether the existence of the canal can be justified on the ground that nearly half the population covered are making at least some use of the canal.

(e) Overall reaction

Finally, after the lapse of 30 years as people look back at all that has happened, their overall reaction towards the Roro Canal Irrigation Project was expressed by 484 persons as follows :

267 (55%)	feel cheated by the government, and
209 (43%)	said that given the very inadequate benefit from the canal, the whole project was not justified.
only 8 (2%)	feel it was justified.

Clubbing the first two responses together, 98% of the people who gave their land for the purpose of the canal with certain hopes and expectations, now feel cheated and question the very existence of the canal. Significantly, the 2% who say the canal project is justified, are the more well-to-do farmers living close to Chaibasa where the canal has at least some water during most parts of the year.

What these 98% of the people will decide to do after they come to know the findings of this study will be something very interesting to watch.

(f) *Government's use of the canal-land for housing colonies :*

The land of the local (mostly adivasi) people is acquired by the government with the promise of providing irrigation... the canal is dug... 30 years pass... as many as 90% of those who gave their land have drawn no benefit in terms of irrigation...

And what do they see now? Housing colonies have quietly been constructed by the government on the land acquired for canal purpose; and those who have been housed there are the government servants and their families who are mostly non-tribals hailing from north Bihar. There cannot be a greater insult to the local tribal people than this. 531 persons expressed their reactions as follows :

287 (54%) stated that it was an unjust use of their land,

27 (05%) said the government had its vested interests even in carrying out its development programmes,

127 (24%) thought that it makes it clear that the government was basically against the tribal people, and

90 (17%) said that the government's action was highly objectionable and that it had a hidden agenda in implementing seemingly neutral projects.

So, cent percent of the people spoken to as part of this study are unanimous in condemning the government for its covert action of settling non-tribal petty government servants and their families right in their midst and in that very land which they gave to the government with the hope of getting some irrigation facilities. The viciousness of the government is on two counts :

(1) Individual non-tribals cannot legally buy tribal land; this obstacle has been overcome by making it look like a government project.

(2) The non-tribal north Biharis generally look down upon the tribal people and have been their exploiters all along.

To take the land of the tribal people in the guise of a development project and install their oppressors in that very land is the height of insult that the government had perpetrated on the tribal people.

(g) Collection of Tax

The other outrageous fact is that despite the canal being dysfunctional in terms of irrigation and 90% of the people not having any benefit thereof, *the local government has been collecting land tax and water tax from the people including for the land which was taken away from them 30 years ago.* The survey findings reveal that 12 households in Chaibasa Block, 52 in Khuntpani and 5 in Seraikela are still paying the land tax ("malgujari") to the government. Several other households were also paying this land tax initially but once they realised that tax was being collected for the land which had been acquired for the canal, they declined to pay it. Another significant thing to note is that the number of households still paying land tax for their alienated land is much less in Chaibasa and Seraikela Blocks because people in general and the younger generation in particular, have become more knowledgeable about the state of affairs and have had the courage to tell the government servants that they would no more pay the tax; whereas the people of Khuntpani Block who are living in interior villages where much less education has taken place, have not picked up enough courage to say no to paying the tax. Where all this illegally collected money goes is still another vexing question.

A word must be said about the government's custom of declaring the entire area as "irrigated" where irrigation through canals has penetrated, and levy water tax from all the farmers irrespective of whether they are in fact using the water or not. While there may be a certain rationale in this practice, it is still questionable as to whether it is justifiable where only a miniscule 3% of the population really benefits from it. Further, the fact that an increasing number of households have stopped paying the water tax and the local administration has willingly accepted the people's refusal to pay the tax only confirms the lacunae in this practice.

(h) The present reality

A final question posed to the people was how they felt about the whole process, focusing particularly on the government's assurance of providing irrigation and on that basis acquiring their land on the one hand, and the present reality on the other. 534 opinions were expressed in this regard :

239 (44.5%)	felt that the whole project betrays the government's real attitude towards the small farmers, namely, it was bent on weakening them by alienating their most basic assets.
215 (40%)	said that the government was finally showing its true colours with regard to the tribal people in general and tribal farmers in particular, and
77 (14%)	expressed the opinion that the govrnment's real intention is alienation of tribal land through whatever means possible, and neutral - looking development projects are one such effective means.

All the above three categories of opinion, however, basically say the same thing, namely, the district-level government bureaucracy is predominantly composed of non-tribal north Biharis who have no sympathy whatever for the tribal people of Jharkhand. Rather most of them would loot whatever they can during their tenure there.

The so-called 'development programmes' executed in the Jharkhand region are really not meant to be of benefit to the Jharkhandi people but mere opportunities to siphon off as much money of the project as possible, and everybody from top to bottom has a share in the cake. With so much corruption as part of the government machinery and its functioning, many schemes are left incomplete and even those that are physically complete are technically faulty and therefore dysfunctional. This is true with regard to any department of the local administration.

All this indicates the fact that the government is not serious in developing the irrigational facilities for the Jharkhandi people of Singhbhum. What is also certain is that whether the projects are completed but dysfunctional or they have been given up half way because of lack of funds, the land of the people measuring several thousands of acres has been alienated from them.

Based on an unpublished paper by Mr. Stan Lurdswami for the Jharkhandi organisation for HumanRights. It is being used here with his due permission.

DISPLACEMENT AND THE REHABILITATION POLICY

Samyadip Chatterji

In a paper on Displacement and Rehabilitation Fernandes and Chatterji observed the following: After 45 years of planned development that has displaced millions of people, the Government of India has finally realised the need to formulate a rehabilitation policy for the Displaced Persons (DPs). While this is a positive point, one does not know whether it is done out of conviction or because of pressure from funders like the World Bank. The National Thermal Power Corporation (NTPC) is the only displacing agency to have a rehabilitation policy. And the main reasons it gives for the need for a policy are the danger of delays in the project because of agitations by the DPs if they are not rehabilitated, the difficulty of getting foreign loans without this component etc. But rehabilitation is not mentioned as a right of the DPs.

In that sense the Draft National Policy for Rehabilitation of Persons Displaced as a Consequence of Acquisition of Land is an improvement. It recognises the need to resettle the DPs because they pay the price of development. However, it takes displacement for granted. It can be argued that displacement itself is an offshoot of the present pattern of development. Thus the thinking behind it has to be questioned.

The salient features of the policy

1. The policy begins by stating that "with the advent of the New Economic Policy, it is expected that there will be large scale investments, both on account of internal generation of capital and increased inflow of foreign investments, thereby creating an enhanced demand for land to be provided within a shorter time-span in an

increasingly competitive market ruled economic structure".

2. It points out that most of India's mineral resources, including coal, iron ore and manganese are located in remote backward areas inhabited by tribals. It further states, that due to the locational advantages and mineral resource base a strong industrial network has been created in these areas implying a cycle of positive growth.

3. Another point that the policy acknowledges is the fact that the demand for land may be for thousands of acres for industry, mega-projects, dams, wild life sanctuaries, reservation of forests, mining projects, Govt. offices and for charitable institutions. It also points out that these lands may be acquired through the acquisition legislations or purchased directly from the land-owners. Whatever might be the case, the process brings in its wake hardships to the person whose lands contribute to the process of growth.

The need for a Rehabilitation Policy

The need for a rehabilitation policy is described by the National Policy statement in the following way:

1. The developmental projects raise questions of equity, fairness, justice and equality before the law, in the matter of distribution of benefits and burdens. Today the project affected people are no longer in a mood to suffer displacement along with its concomitant attributes like occupational degeneration, social disorientation, pauperisation, loss of dignity and often getting cheated of the compensation which serve to make the experience a trauma. This has given rise to protest movements, marked by a growing militancy.

2. An interesting feature of the growing protest movement has been the creation of a national

awareness of the problem. The Press, the activist groups, the social workers and the judiciary have combined together to not only educate the masses about the problem but also to build up a national consciousness. The refrain has also been taken up by the political parties and even by the international organisations to give to it a wider than national connotation. The international conference of nations on Environment at Rio de Janeiro in 1992 has served sufficiently to internationalise the issue. The world financial institutions can go to the extent of withholding loan and aid so as to get fulfilment for its ecological concerns (Sardar Sarovar Project).

Constitutional Perspective

Constitutional perspective which is related to the problem of displacement and resettlement as seen by the policy refers to Schedule VII of the Constitution of India, Article 19 (i) (e) of the Constitution and the decision of the judiciary in relation to various cases related to this issue. The policy also refers to human rights and international law, the universal declaration of human rights, the two declarations of political and civil rights as well as the I.L.O revised section 107.

All these factors make it imperative according to the policy to formulate a comprehensive National Policy on Rehabilitation of Displaced persons as a consequence of acquisition of Land.

PRINCIPLES GOVERNING REHABILITATION

1. The draft mentions that the principle of "total rehabilitation" should be adopted in the rehabilitation policy. By this it means to synchronize the rehabilitation programme with the project implementation. As soon as the project is notified the project authorities should take immediate measures for chalking out a detailed rehabilitation programme. Further, the

rehabilitation programme must be multi-dimensional. It should not only extend to financial compensation but also include social, economic, educational, environmental, physical, occupational and cultural aspects as well.

2. It is mentioned in the policy that the aim of the rehabilitation policy should be to minimise the hardship that the DPs face on being displaced. For this, the policy recommends that resettlement must provide not only shelter and food but also their new place of resettlement must have access to income generating systems, communications as well as infrastructure not inferior to that of their original habitat within a reasonable period of time, say not more than three years.

3. It is stated in the policy that there should be no displacement of people without rehabilitation being completed. It further mentions that even if the people are required to shift it must be with their full consent and understanding, also there should be a close link between the construction schedule and the critical steps being taken for resettlement.

4. The draft talks about compensating the DPs for all their losses suffered due to displacement. The draft states that the resettlement site and the resource base should be large enough to accommodate natural growth in population and to generate incomes to provide for a progressive rise in standard of living.

5. The draft lays down that the displaced persons who are to be resettled in already settled communities, must be resettled in such a manner that they are integrated with the host community on the basis of equality, mutual respect and understanding. This must be consistent with the desire of each community to preserve its own identity and culture.

Stages of Rehabilitation

Land Assessment

1. The policy states categorically that in the past there has been a tendency to acquire more land than what is actually required. The explanation it gives for this phenomenon is that more land is acquired due to the requirement of land. The other reason it gives is that land value is always subject to appreciation and it forms a sizable part of the capital assets at the time of future equity reconstruction.

2. The draft states that before any kind of rehabilitation formulation is done it shall be necessary to assess the impact of the project upon the number of persons to be displaced. It further states that this assessment must be undertaken by an authority independent of the project authorities except in the case of defence projects where impact assessment will be undertaken by the defence authorities themselves.

3. Another salient feature of the draft is that it acknowledges the superiority of the Land Acquisition Act, 1894. It declares that all land shall be acquired by the provisions of the Land Acquisition Act. The draft points out that the State Govts. should fix existing land price in the nearest command area of developed irrigation projects which should be the basis of calculation for compensation in the case of tribals.

Land for Land Basis

The draft points out that land on one to one basis is an ideal but not always feasible. It states that most of the government's land already stands distributed. Acquisition of land for this purpose would mean further displacement. Hence, the Implementation Committee of

the Project/State Govt. should provide land to such displaced persons, who have been exclusively dependent upon agriculture on a proportionate basis, to the extent feasible, with preference to
the members of the Scheduled Castes/Scheduled Tribes, and other weaker sections of the
society.

Grants and Amenities

Resettlement Grant

1. The draft lays down that a fixed sum would be paid as a resettlement grant per displaced family as the cost for dismantling of house, transportation of the house-hold kits etc. In the case of tribals an ex-gratia amount of rupees 30,000 may be given to each tribal towards the cost of construction in addition to free house plots.

2. It also mentions that where neither land nor job has been provided to the DPs, the head of each displaced family should be provided with a subsistence allowance in the form of a resettlement grant on a monthly basis subject to the maximum of rupees 1000 per month for a period of twenty years or till alternative employment has been found.

Job Planning

1. It has been the experience that many a times even the employment that is available in the unskilled, semi-skilled and clerical categories have been denied to the displaced persons on grounds of being wanting in requisite qualifications. A thorough advance job-planning would hence be necessary for absorption of the displaced manpower. Income generation scheme need to be formulated with reference to the poverty profile of the affected villages and the perspective of the host community.

2. The ancillaries/subsidiaries to be set up will also be required to bear the burden of providing direct employment to the Displaced Persons.

3. The exercise in job-planning should be completed before the requisition is filed for acquisition of lands.

4. As a matter of principle, jobs in unskilled and semi-skilled categories should be reserved for members of the displaced families and priority may be given to them in class III and class IV jobs in the Project. First preference should be given to the Scheduled Tribes and Scheduled Castes.

5. There should be relaxation in the qualifications relating to the semi-skilled/unskilled jobs.

6. All the displaced persons, deprived of their means of livelihood in any form and in any manner and who are not otherwise compensated and resettled should be provided with jobs within a reasonable distance from the place of resettlement.

Technical Education and Training

1. It shall be the responsibility of the Project Authorities to impart the necessary technical skill to the eligible displaced persons.

2. In large Projects where the displacement is of a high order the Project should open its own technical schools/institutes for this purpose or get seats reserved for them in private institutes.

3. The contractors may be compelled to employ the displaced persons. This will have the added advantage that jobs will be available even from the pre-construction stage in survey etc. and the displaced persons will feel emotionally involved with the Project.

Self-Employment

1. The role of self-employment in rehabilitation of the displaced persons assumes critical proportions. It certainly serves to create adequate opportunities for down stream employment. All such openings will be fully explored and listed in the job plan.

2. The persons who do not otherwise qualify for direct employment or collateral employment will have to be settled for such self- employment.

3. In exceptionally large projects, independent entrepreneurship and self-employment schools can be started.

4. Preference should be given to the displaced persons in matters like allotment of shops, business sites, raw materials, finished materials like yarns etc. for further business.

5. In matters of supply of raw materials, allotment of contracts for some special type of work not requiring high skill, preference should be given to the displaced persons.

6. The Employment Cell will also have to act as a forum for procuring loans from financial institutions to the displaced persons for self-employment and arrange for suitable technical advice and guidance for self-employment.

Rehabilitation Site

1. Whenever a project displaces tribals, such communities should preferably be resettled in a zone adjacent to the affected area comparable with the previous socio-cultural, linguistic and economic characteristics of the community.

2. Tribal communities should be strictly settled in the

areas of their choice. They should be enabled to exercise their choice by furnishing them with full information regarding the resettlement sites and providing opportunities for physical inspection. Even forest areas could be made available to settle the tribals by suitably amending the provisions of the relevant forest conservation laws.

3. The resettlement sites should be inspected by the Implementation Committee and by the members of the organisations of Displaced Persons and approved by them.

4. Every person should be allotted free of cost a minimum of 85 sq. metres of land in urban areas and minimum 500 sq. metres of land in rural areas for homestead in the new settlement. Where multi-storeyed buildings are constructed for housing the displaced persons in urban areas, flats measuring a corresponding built-up area of 85 sq. metres or its equivalent in the built-up space should be given.

5. Separate house-sites should be allotted to major sons in family, persons living on Govt. land, on land belonging to other landholders, landless labourers living on land of the landholders to whom they are attached etc. This would be applicable to tribals only. In case of non-tribals the States may decide on the allotment of house-sites to such categories of persons.

6. The Project should make provision for construction of houses which should not have a living space less than that previously occupied.

7. The plan for construction should more or less follow the old pattern of the village and for executing the construction plan, technical input would be made available by the Building Centres being set up at district level.

8. The beneficiaries wherever possible should be

allowed to make the construction themselves, for which, they shall be paid wages. However, if they so like, they may contribute additionally for materials for a larger or better house.

9. The places of religious worship etc. should be built at the Project cost at the same scale.

10. Land should be earmarked for traditional tribal institutions.

Civic Amenities

1. The basic idea behind total rehabilitation is to provide a quality of life superior to that enjoyed by the displaced persons so as to reduce the trauma involved in displacement. The following yardsticks of civic amenities have been deemed necessary for the purpose:-

   (a) One primary school (3 rooms) for 100 families.

   (b) One Panchayat ghar for every 500 families.

   (c) One dispensary for every 500 families.

   (d) One seed store for every 500 families.

   (e) One children's park for every 500 families.

   (f) One village pond for every 500 families.

   (g) Drinking water source for every 50 families.

   (h) Each colony should be linked to main road by roads of appropriate standard.

   (i) One platform for every 50 families.

   (j) In addition a provision of 30% additional area for roads. Government buildings, open space etc. shall be made under civic amenities.

THE NTPC POLICY

Regarding the definition of displaced persons the NTPC policy divides them into two broad categories namely oustees and evictees .

Oustees as well as their sub-categories are defined as:

> "Persons who reside and own land or homesteads in the area to be acquired. In a joint family or in case of joint holdings, every married or unmarried major who has a share in the land as per Hindu Joint Family Act will be considered as an oustee".

The Sub-categories of oustees can be:

i. ***Substantially Affected Person (SAP)***

a) An oustee whose more than 1/3 of land is to be acquired and is left with less than 2 Ha of land after acquisition.

b) An oustee who will be left with 1 Ha or less of land.

ii. ***Homestead Oustee***

A person whose homestead is to be acquired although no land has been acquired.

iii. ***Absentee Landlord***

An oustee person who is not an occupant of the land for 5 years prior to the notification under Section 4 of the Land Acquisition Act. The principal earning of an absentee landlord should also be through some source other than the land being acquired."

B. *Evictee*

Evictees as well as their sub categories are defined as:

"Persons who derive their income from the land and reside in the area to be acquired but do not have legal title either to the land or the homestead. The following categories of persons can be considered under this group:

i. A tenant (tiller) who is in actual possession of land under relevant tenancy law.

ii. An Agricultural labourer who does not have land but earns his living principally through manual labour on that land.

iii. A tribal residing in the forest land.

iv. A landless labourer cultivating government land".

Eligibility Status

Eligibility of persons who will be rehabilitated are divided into the following categories:

The table below indicates the status of each category of persons or families with respect to compensation and rehabilitation.

Categories of Person	*Rehabilitation*
A. Oustee	

I.	Substantially affected Person (SAP)	Eligible
ii.	Absentee landlord	Not Eligible
iii.	Homestead Oustee with infrastructural facilities.	Only home sites could be provided
iv.	Homestead oustee occupying Govt. land	-do-
B.	Evictee	
i.	Tiller tenant	Eligible
ii.	Agricultural labour working on private land	Eligible
iii.	Agricultural labour cultivating Govt. land	Eligible
iv.	Tribals residing in forest land proposed for acquisition	Eligible

It appears that the present NTPC policy is an improvement on the earlier NTPC guidelines in that the former includes tillers and landless labourers who are now eligible for rehabilitation.

Content of the Rehabilitation Policy

Land for land

The land for land policy is similar to the National Policy. It stipulates that the NTPC would negotiate with the State Governments for free release of reserve land for allotment to the SAP, "not exceeding the extent of land lost or 5 acres of land whichever is less. For example, if one acre is acquired the oustee will be provided one acre with no cash compensation. If say ten acres is acquired, the oustee will be provided five acres of land and cash compensation for the balance five acres".

COAL INDIA POLICY

Objectives

The resettlement and rehabilitation policies followed by the subsidiaries have evolved overtime and undergone numerous changes in response to changing circumstances. As and when the Central or state Governments issue new guidelines for resettlement and rehabilitation, Coal India will review and modify its resettlement and rehabilitation policy taking into account the changing conditions in coal producing areas. However, as a matter of principle, the compensation and benefits offered to the people affected by Coal India will be at least equal to and not less than those prescribed by the laws and guidelines of the central and state governments. However, in any case Coal India's resettlement and rehabilitation policy has to be approved by the Ministry of Coal.

In the light of the growing difficulties many subsidiaries face in land acquisition highest priority will be given to avoid or minimize disturbance of the local population. In their decisions to open new mines or expand existing ones, subsidiaries will explore alternative sites and project designs in order to minimize the need of resettlement. Wherever people are likely to be adversely affected by the project, the subsidiaries will prepare resettlement and rehabilitation action plans for the project.

Minimizing the need for Resettlement

Transition period between acquisition of land and actual resettlement has to be minimized so that the DPs may be able to not only regain their standard of living but also improve it.

Coal India Policy speaks of working closely with the NGOs which are legally recognised in the preparation and implementation of rehabilitation plan. The National Policy also speaks of similar cooperation after displacement has been affected. However the maximum amount of land allotment could be limited to five acres to a family.

Coal India's Definition of Project Affected Persons

Coal India Policy considers adult individuals as the unit of entitlement. It divides the wide range of PAPs into two major categories.

A. Landowners including those owning Govt. settled land including Tribals cultivating land under traditional rights; persons owning homesteads and persons from whom both land and their homestead are acquired.

B. The landless such as sharecroppers, tenants, day labourers; tribals dependent on forest produce and persons whose homestead is acquired.

Compensation and Rehabilitation Policy of Coal India

The compensation and rehabilitation options are as follows:

(a). All land owners with titles including tribals cultivating land under traditional rights will receive monetary compensation, the value of land being determined on the basis of prevailing legal norms. In addition the subsidiaries will offer, if feasible, employment as per their own policies.

(b). The PAPs will identify and purchase with the assistance of the subsidiaries of Coal India equivalent replacement of land using their land compensation.

(c). The subsidiaries will assist a PAP to establish non- farm self-employment through the provision of infrastructure or co-operatives.

(d). A PAP with less than two acres of land will receive assistance in the form of a subsistence allowance or grant for productive investment provided his income does not exceed Rs. 12,000 per annum.

Critique of the above Policies

The State of Displacement

The figure of 145 lakh DPs between 1951 and 1985 given in the draft is the conservative estimate which was made in 1989 of those displaced by dams, mines, industries and wildlife sanctuaries (Fernandes, Das and Rao 1989: 89-91). By extrapolating more recent data and through better analysis, Fernandes et al. have now arrived at an estimate of 213 lakh DPs till 1990 (see Table). This, to the best of our knowledge, is the only comprehensive estimate of displacement in India. That gives the first feature of displacement. Though millions have been displaced in the name of national development, no reliable database exists on the extent of displacement and rehabilitation. It is a sign of the decision-makers' lack of commitment to rehabilitate the DPs. No rehabilitation is possible without knowing the number and type of DPs. But hardly any project gives accurate data. Even in the famous Sardar Sarovar, the official figures for DPs range from 45,000 (NCA 1986: 2&5)) to 90,000 (Babbar 1992). Other estimates range from 70,000 (Datta and De Roy 1986: 14) and 108,000 (NIUA n.d.: 6) DPs by the dam alone to 175,000 by the dam and canals together (Morse and Berger 1992). The situation gets worse when it comes to less known projects. For example, the original plan of the Farakka Superthermal Plant mentioned neither displacement nor resettlement. Today the World Bank (1994: 2/6) puts the number of its DPs at around 50,000.

Table: A Conservative Estimate of Persons Displaced by Various Categories of Projects, 1951-1990

Sl.No.	*Type of Project*	*Total Dps No.*	*Rehabilitated*	*Backlog*
01.	Mines	25,50,000	6,30,000	19,20,000
02.	Dams	1,64,00,000	41,00,000	-
03.	Industries	12,50,000	3,75,000	8,75,000
04.	Wildlife	6,00,000	1,25,000	4,75,000
05.	Others	5,00,000	1,50,000	3,50,000
Total		**2,13,00,000**	**53,80,000**	**1,59,20,000**

Source : Fernandes 1994:24

The state of rehabilitation is a more obvious sign of lack of commitment to the DPs. According to estimates fewer than 30 per cent of those displaced in the 1950s and 1960s had been resettled till 1980 (Hansda 1983: 23). Studies show that the situation has not changed substantially in the 1980s (Mahapatra 1990: 91-92), particularly in the case of the marginalised like the tribals and dalits. For example, Gujarat and Maharashtra have a "land for land" policy for DPs of irrigation projects. Only 15.4 per cent of the tribal DPs and 31.4 per cent of the others entitled to it have got its benefits (Fernandez 1990: 36). The country that has displaced millions of people does not till now have a rehabilitation policy, leave alone a law.

That is not surprising because most DPs belong to the weaker sections. According to an estimate more than 40 per cent of the pre-1990 DPs and at least 50 per cent today are tribals (Fernandes 1994: 32) who form only 7.85 per cent of the country's population. Dalits are probably around 20 per cent (Mahapatra 1990: 90). The tribals depend on common property resources (CPRs) like forests and community land that the present law considers government property. As such no compensation is paid to them. Besides, the regions they inhabit have been administratively neglected and, as a consequence, considered backward. Since compensation is based on the market price, the amount they get for the land lost is too low for them to begin a new life after being deprived of their livelihood. Most dalits, being landless agricultural labourers or other service castes, depend for a living on land owned by others. But only patta holders are compensated and the landless ignored (Dhagamwar 1989: 176).

The Issues Around Rehabilitation

From the situation of displacement one can identify the norms on which a rehabilitation policy should be based. The first is decision-making concerning displacement. In a country that calls itself democratic, can people be deprived of their livelihood without their intelligent involvement in the decision? Till now no project has recognised this right. The assumption is that the people, most of them poor and powerless, should adjust themselves to the situation once a decision to displace them is taken (Baxi 1989).

The second concerns CPRs. India has two types of citizens. Those encroaching on revenue land may become its owners after some years. But those in possession of forest land can never be patta holders even though their ancestors might have been in possession for centuries before the present colonial law came into force (Singh 1989: 96). Thus India follows the principle of terra nullius i.e. that common land not having individual ownership documents belongs to no one. The White colonialists followed this principle in occupying indigenous lands in Australia, New Zealand, Southern Africa and the Americas (Cockburn 1993). In India it is called eminent domain and continues to be the guiding principle in land transactions. CPRs that are the tribal life support system, are assumed to be State property and not compensated. The landless who depend on the village as a community have no right to be compensated for the loss of their livelihood.

Some go beyond compensation to question the ownership pattern itself. Is the project to be owned only by those who invest capital? Should not the DPs who are deprived of their livelihood be partners and shareholders in the project? They would have to be given adequate training to be involved in the decisions concerning the project and may have to get professional managers to run it. But it has to be their decision because they, as a community, own CPRs (Sharma 1993).

Eminent domain has implications for the cost-benefit analysis and compensation. Only the marketable commodities of the formal economy are taken into consideration while calculating cost-benefit within the planning commission criterion of 1:1.5. Though the DPs lose their livelihood, the informal economy to which most of them belong, is ignored and only the market value of their individually owned property is compensated. The few studies available on this question indicate that if the informal benefits from CPRs and even individual land, and the loss of livelihood were taken into consideration, very few projects would see the light of day according to the planning commission norms (Fernandes and Raj 1992).

To this question is linked the search for alternatives. It is an obligation in justice for the decision-makers to consider non-displacing alternatives before opting for projects that displace people. One sees no sign of such an approach to decision-making. For example, many sites may be thought of for a major dam. But alternatives to the dam itself do not form part of the decision-making process.

Nor does the question of who gets the benefits. Displacement in the name of national development has become a mode of transferring CPRs from the communities to whom they are a life support system to the corporate sector to whom they are a source of profit or raw material to produce consumer goods for the middle class (Sharma 1978: 60). Thus a clear distinction exists between the class that gets the benefits and those who pay the price of national development. The powerless categories like the tribals and dalits, particularly women among them, are the losers.

Finally, there should be no displacement without rehabilitation being an integral part of the project. Its cost should be included in the project. In reality, when included in the scheme, it is viewed as a concession, not a right of the DPs. Its cost is rarely included in the project. Often the budget of IRDP and other welfare programmes is diverted for it. In most cases only the economic component is taken into consideration. That the DPs, most of them illiterate and inadequately exposed to the formal economy, are pushed overnight, with no transition, from a sustenance to a competitive economy is forgotten. For example, the decision on projects like Sardar Sarovar and NALCO (Orissa) was taken in the 1960s and construction began in the 1980s. During this 20-year period no effort was made to make the DPs literate, impart to them job-oriented skills or to deal with the psychological trauma of forced eviction. Most jobs go to outsiders. The DPs are not compensated for the psychological trauma and pain they suffer.

The Koel Karo Project - A Case Study

About 1,50,000 indigenous (tribal and semi-tribal) people of Ranchi and Gumla districts of the Jharkhand region of Bihar have been living under a constant threat of being displaced from their homes and ancestral land for more than 35 years, owing to the proposed Koel - Karo Hydro - electricity Project. They were subjected to this apparently unending agony way back in 1959 when the project was first taken up by the Government of Bihar under the Bihar Electricity Board. Inspite of the strong resistance from the people and opposition from the environmentalists, scientists and social workers the government of Bihar in connivance with the Central government has been waging what can be termed as a " psychological war " against the helpless tribal people by keeping the threat alive all these years without any rhyme or reason. Every time when it appears that the government is going to abandon the project, as it happened in the late '70s and early '90s, the state government of Bihar comes back with it with a renewed vigour and a new set of promises for the people. This year also the people are experiencing the same threat looming large over them with the declaration of the Bihar government to begin the implementation work of the project immediately. The Central government has already agreed to sanction Rs. 10 crores to this effect.

Mr. Laloo Prasad Yadav, Chief Minister of Bihar, after a consultation with the Union Power Minister Mr. N. K. P. Salve in New Delhi declared on the 21st of May 95, that the foundation-stone-laying ceremony would be held on 5th of July 1995 in Lohajimi, the proposed site of the Karo dam in Ranchi district. According to him Mr. P. V. Narsimha Rao, Prime Minister of India, agreed to lay the foundation stone . The news spread like an unwarranted shock to the people. The local news papers immediately started carrying news favouring the implementation of the project which left a demoralising effect on the minds of the people. All the national political parties released statements supporting the move of the Bihar Government, several non-tribal organisations followed suit. Even to the people's dismay and disgust the Jharkhand Mukti Morcha (JMM) declared its support to the project. After a short spell of confusion, however, the affected people under the banner of Koel-Karo Jan Sangathan (KKJS) reorganised themselves and a huge rally was held in Torpa on 10th June, 1995 to mark the protest. Their moral was highly boosted on the previous day when several socio-cultural and youth organisations expressed their solidarity with the KKJS and strongly condemned the decision of the government on the occasion of Birsa Munda's Martyr's day observation on the 9th. On 9th June a joint meeting of the 19 Jharkhandi social organisations and political parties were held in Ranchi where a joint strategy of oppose the project was chalked out. The All Jharkhand Students Union and the Jharkhand People's Party jointly called an 'All Jharkhand Bandh' on 5th July to prevent the Prime Minister from entering the region. Jharkhand Visthapit Mukhti Sangh and the Jharkhandis Organisation for Human Rights (JOHAR) declared that they would organise thousand of men to lie down on the roads leading to Lohajimi near Tapkara, the proposed site for laying the foundation stone, and in case the PM still insists the women would strip before the PM to show their dismay. A public meeting was organised by the KKJS on 21st June in Torpa followed by another on 26th in Topkara. In the Koel region in Gumla district people reciprocated soon by holding a huge rally in Basia on 29th June. The same day the Bihar Chief Minister Laloo Prasad Yadav declared in the Assembly that in the event of the Prime Minister's inability to turn up he himself would lay the foundation stone. This enraged the people further and they took it as a challenge. A ten thousand strong protest march was held on 30th June in Jaipur. A 'Janta Curfew' was clamped by the KKJS through out the region from 1st July and the agitators blocked all roads leading to the Karo dam site. On 2nd July the Union Energy Minister Mr. N.K.P. Salve asked the Bihar Chief Minister to postpone the much condemned Foundation Stone Laying Ceremony. A mammoth gathering of the people celebrated the victory of the people on the 5th in Torpa and the rest of Jharkhand observed a successful Bandh.

The Project

The Koel - Karo Hydro Electric Project was mooted in 1959 with a view to fulfil the increasing demand of electricity by the growing industrial units in eastern India. The plan was drawn for maximum utilisation of the water of the river South Koel and its tributary North Karo for the generation of power. The initial proposal was to generate 710 mega watt of electricity. With this end the construction of two dams was proposed, one with a height of 44 mt. near Basia in Gumla district, and the other, with a height of 55 m. near Lohajimi in Ranchi district . These two dams were to be connected to each other by a 34.7 km. long underground tunnel so that the water accumulated in the Basia dam could be diverted to the dam in Lohajimi. Two underground power stations were proposed to be constructed, one in Lapungkhel with 6 units of 115 mega watt each and the other in Raitoli with 20 mega watt. The electricity produced by them would be brought to Patratu and Chandil, in Hazaribagh and East Singhbhum districts respectively for the Eastern grid.

It was estimated that for the completion of the

project altogather 50,000 acres of land was to be acquired, of which 25-30 thousand acres were mostly agricultural fields belonging to the tribal and semi-tribal communities, and the rest was forest land on which tribal people had been enjoying traditional and legal rights. About 10,739 families were estimated to be evicted by the project, 85-90% of them tribal, from 122 villages. According to a non-governmental survey, however, the number of villages to be affected are 256 and about one and a half lakh people would be displaced. The cost of the project was estimated at Rs. 390.40 crores which has now increased to Rs. 1750 crores. A non-governmental estimate tells us that possibly the real cost is 2100 crore Rupees.

Progress of the Project

The government of Bihar prepared a grand plan of generating Hydro- electricity by using the water of all the big rivers of the state in the '50s. The Koel-Karo Project was a part of it. The Bihar state Electricity Board took 15 years to complete a survey work for the project in collaboration with the National Hydro-electric Power Corporation (NHPC). Immediately after that land was acquired for the construction of roads and other purposes to accelerate the work of the project implementation. However, the government of Bihar did not set any time frame for the completion of the project. Time passed by without any progress in the work of the project . The government did nothing except running offices in Ranchi and Torpa.

In 1980-81 the government of Bihar handed over the responsibility of the implementation of the project to the National Hydro-electric Power Corporation, a Government of India undertaking. The NHPC prepared a time-bound programme of seven years to implement the project. But nothing was done, except for the construction of a bridge over the river Karo near the Lohajimi dam site, till 1994. Meanwhile the Government received Environment clearance in 1982 and Forest clearance in July 1990.

People's Resistance

The project affected people were kept in the dark till '73 about the details of the project. They , however, knew about the project and the impending threat to their lives and future. After the completion of the survey in '73 the Bihar Electricity Board started sending government officials to the sites to initiate the process of land acquisition. The people became alert immediately and organised themselves .They formed the "Jan Sanyojan Samity" in the Koel region and the "Jan Sangharsh Samity" in the Karo area. Both the organisations demanded details of the project to be made public by the government. Realising the need of stronger unity of the affected people of the two river valleys they merged the two organisations into "Koel-Karo Jan Sanghatan" in 1976. Thereafter a memorandum was prepared and submitted to the government . It contained the willingness of the people to accept the project provided that the government clarifies its principle in consultation with the project affected people (PAPs). The Govt. till date has not replied to this demand.

The way the work of the project progressed revealed its futility. At one point the NEPC even advised the government to give it up altogether. In the following years the affected people raised the issue of social, cultural and economic rehabilitation.

During 1977-78 the affected people tried to approach the government several times for a patient hearing of their demands. But the government did nothing but lending a deaf ear to it and the project work went on unabated. Out of frustration the KKJS launched a 'stop work' agitation. Roads to the proposed dam site in Tapkara were blocked and several demonstrations and rallies were organised. this compelled the government to call a tripartite meting which included the representatives of the KKJS, the NEPC and the Government of Bihar. As an outcome of this a questionnaire was prepared which was to be filled in by door-to-door visit of the project affected people. The purpose was to know the opinion of the people regarding the project. After covering three villages, however, the programme was abandoned. Thus once again the government lost the chance of getting the confidence of the people. Thereafter the KKJS prepared a 16 point charter of demands and presented it to the government. It highlighted the interdependence of the social, cultural and economic aspects of the tribal life and the need for a holistic rehabilitation policy. But the government blatantly ignored the demand and unilaterally declared the rate of financial compensation. At this point the people proposed that the government should take up two villages to set an example of proper rehabilitation as was promised by it, and if it turned out to be a satisfactory one they would accept the rehabilitation package of the government. But the government neither paid heed to the proposal nor clarify its position on socio--cultural and economic rehabilitation.

In 1984 the government of Bihar declared that the project would be implemented by force and accordingly a contingent of armed forces was sent to the Karo area. The following resistance movement was marked by the participation of women in great numbers. People not only drove away the armed forces but also destroyed the office cum go-down in the dam site at Lohajimi. Along side a section of the people approached the Supreme Court. A civil Writ Petition was instituted bearing NO. 13666-67 of 1984 by V. Lakra. It sought to restrain the government from using force to get possession over land till the measures of compensation were comprehensively decided. The Hon'ble Court responded by issuing an injunction prohibiting the government from taking forcible possession over land.

A People's Workshop

A three day workshop on the future of the Koel-Karo agitation in the context of the general problems of displacement of people due to large and small development projects introduced by the government of India was jointly organised by the All Jharkhand Student's

Union and the Subaltern Consultants Trust in Torpa from 12th to 14th November, 1995.

The workshop was attended by 50 odd village representatives of the proposed submerging area of the Karo region including the leaders of the movement, such as, Mr. Paulus Guria, the headman (Parah Raja) of the Guria Clan, Mr. Soma Munda, the Mukhia of Lohajimi, Ms. Emani Guria, the leader of Women's Wing of the KKJS, Ms. Dayamani Barla, a fire-brand social activist, Mr. Regan Guria, the leader of the youth wing of the KKJS etc. As resource persons there were Ms. Medha Patkar of the Narmada Bachao Andolan, Ms. Gemma Mendis, of Chotanagpur Adivasi Seva Samity presently leading the movement against displacement due to open-cast coal mining in Hazaribagh, Mr. Allauddin Ansari, representing the displaced people's movement in Giridih, Mr. Xavier Dias and Ms. Ajita Dias, representing displaced people's movement against Jadugora Uranium mining, Mr. Meghnad of Kutku dam movement and Mr. Sanjay Bosu Mullick, President, Jharkhand People's Party. The workshop was also attended by representatives of the Jharkhand Organisation for Human Rights (JOHAR), Movement Against Displacement (MAD) and Bindrai Institute for Research Study and Action (BIRSA). Mr. Damu Banra, General Secretary AJSU, Mr. Lalit Mahato, President, AJSU and Mr. Samyadip Chatterji, Executive Trustee, Subaltern Consultants Trust jointly conducted the workshop.

During the course of discussion the resource persons dealt with the historical perspective of displacement of tribal people in the Jharkhand region. It was shown that with the emergence and subsequent extension of the state (stratified society) the tribal people were dislodged from their habitats time and again through ages. In Jharkhand since the emergence of the state out of non-tribal matrix in the 15th century the ancestral land of the tribal people is being taken over by force or fraudulent means. During the British rule the phenomenon of displacement reached a greater high which was further augmented after independence. According to the resource persons it was one sided development i.e. development favouring the already rich at the cost of the poor and impoverished. Land which rightfully belongs to the tribal society is being used for the prosperity of the non-tribal upper castes and classes and to no advantage to the original settlers. Any opposition to these lopsided developmental schemes is suppressed, at times ruthlessly, on the pretext of national interest. The respondents cited the example of the dams constructed under the Damodar Valley Corporation (DVC) in the 50s. The large scale displacement of the tribal and other indigenous peoples resulted in their total destitution and today the whole region appears to be a desert; all the dams are silted and no electricity is being generated, the cost went much higher than the benefit. Ms. Medha Patkar called for a unified struggle to fight the forces of exploitation which through centuries have been displacing tribal peoples throughout the country. She commented on the effect displacement has on women. They, she said, were the worst affected. The compensation after the displacement is always given to the man of the house, where in fact in tribal communities living in their own environment, it is the woman who looks after the household. She is the person who goes to the forest to collect things necessary for the household and works in the fields more than the man. She denounced strongly the consumerist culture and the forces encouraging such culture for their own benefit. She pointed out the necessity of learning the simple life style of the tribal people.

At the second session of the workshop, the displaced persons spoke about their experiences which they have been facing for several years. One of the participants related a tribal folk tale in which there was a bird in the forest who promise a better future to the other animals in the forest. The bird fools all the animals by saying that they should leave the forest as there was much more prosperity for them elsewhere. All the animals believed this story and left the forest. Finally, it was a crab that the bird transported. The crab clung on to the bird's neck so that he could be flown to this destination. On reaching this place the crab saw that all the other crabs as well as all the other animals of the forest were not happy nor were they able to survive as well as they used to in the forest.

The crab realises that the bird by promising a better future to all the animals had actually displaced them for his own self interest. Once the crab realised this he strangled the bird with his claws. The point this DP was making was that for thousands of years their forest, land, water and culture had been taken away from them by promises of a better future through compensation and other so called "attractive packages". The moral of this tale is to realise the fact of displacement of tribals. The crab in this story signifies a realisation which leads to a struggle of tribal peoples to ensure that they are no longer fooled, and at any cost preserve their culture, land, water and their forests. The bird, signifies the encroacher, the non-adivasi, who has, for thousands of years, exploited these tribal people by the process of land alienation. The outcome of this process has been the alienation of tribal land.

Mr. Paulus Guria, the key speaker representing the point of view of the affected people said that his people were not against 'development' as such. But how long would this blind-race of so-called development go on at the cost of land, forest and water belonging to the tribal people? Will the present concept of development allow a space to accommodate the views and aspirations of the tribal societies? The question Mr. Soma Munda raised was a basic question. He said that the government had lost the confidence of the people of not only Jharkhand but all over the country wherever it implemented big developmental projects. Hundreds of thousands of people, a big chunk of them tribals, were displaced but inspite of lucrative promises an overwhelming majority of them had not yet been rehabilitated. He questioned the integrity of the planners and the implementors. In Jharkhand all the projects so far been implemented provided a lucrative grazing ground for the unholy nexus of the politicians, bureaucrats and the contractors, and thus finally turned out to be burdens on the society instead of being contributing components. Why one should sacrifice oneself for the benefit of a handful of rich and powerful people of the society? he questioned. Ms. Dayamani Barla initiated a discussion on the alternative developmental planning. She said that the construction of big dams could never be a profitable project even if one excluded the human and environmental costs. However big the compensation package might be, the loss the tibal people would incur would never be compensated. The possibility of constructing a number of small dams on the same rivers instead of a single big one with the same objective should be given serious thought, she added.

After having prolonged discussion the participants came up with the following resolutions.

1. Considering the opinion of the people the Koel-Karo Hydro-Electric Project should be dropped forever without further delay.

2. The government should not sanction any project without receiving the consent of the affected people through a proper interaction with them.

3. The government should make all the details of the proposed project available to the affected people well in advance before initiating dialogue with them.

4. In the event of receiving the people's consent the government should complete the rehabilitation programme and settle the financial compensation to the fullest satisfaction of the displaced people and only after that the project work should begin.

5. In the event of rejection of the project by the people the government should not on any pretext use force to make people accept it.

6. The government should drop all the big dam construction projects and ask the planning commission to explore alternative sources for the

generation of power.

Conclusion

The people facing displacement have now realised that they need to retaliate trough dialogue as well as struggle against this sought of oppression. They are clear on the point that they are no longer going to sacrifice their lands for a wrong and unequal concept of development.

The story narrated above clearly shows that there is an understanding that the DP's have been hood winked for several centuries by the dominant upper sections of our society, namely the upper castes. Today, it is known to them that their lands, forest, water, culture and identity is a basic fundamental right to be different and to be human.

As the new century dawns upon us, the indigenous people through struggle and conviction will be prepared to face the new challenges brought on by new developmental projects introduced by the liberalization policy of the Government of India. They know that they must struggle against these displacing projects as well as those who are the brains behind them.

They are no longer interested in compromise, on the other hand have an ideology of creating alternatives against displacement through self-rule and self-determination.

There is a feeling among DPs and many government as well as non-government agencies that displacement is to be taken for granted and a comprehensive rehabilitation policy is the remedy. This is a factor one must evaluate. We believe that displacement of people is a crime committed by the State on its citizens. There are alternative means of development in this era. One does not have to displace people in the name of development. People lose their livelihood for whose development?

References

Chatterji, Samyadip &Fernandes, Walter 1995. A Critique of the Draft National Policy for Rehabilitation of Persons Displaced as a Consequence of Acquisationof Land. Published in Lokayan Bulletin March-April 1996, CAPART Bullietin and Legal News and Views, ISI, New Delhi.

Areeparampil, Mathew. 1989. "Industries, Mines and Dispossession of Indigenous Peoples: The Case of Chotanagpur," in Walter Fernandes and Enakshi Ganguly Thukral (eds). *Development, Displacement and Rehabilitation: Issues for a National Debate.* New Delhi: Indian Social Institute, pp. 13-38.

Babbar, Vinod. 1992. " Land Acquisition and Transfer: National and Sectoral Resettlement Policies, Participatory Approaches." Paper presented at the World Bank and Electrobras Sponsored *Conference on Resettlement in Power Projects.* Santa Catarina: May 4-14.

Baxi, Upendra. 1989. "Notes on Constitutional and Legal Aspects of Rehabilitation and Displacement," in Walter Fernandes and Enakshi Ganguly Thukral (eds). op. cit. pp. 164-170.

Cockburn, Robert. 1993. "Years after Cook's `Misadventure'," *The Statesman* (New Delhi), June 19.

CPR. 1985. *People's Participation as a Key to Himalayan Ecosystem Development.* New Delhi: Centre for Policy Research.

Datta, Chandan and Rashmi De Roy. 1986. *Big Dams on the Narmada, Vol. II.* New Delhi: Environment Services Group, Worldwide Fund Nature-India.

Dhagamwar, Vasudha. 1989. "Rehabilitation: Policy and Institutional Changes Required," in Walter Fernandes and Enakshi Ganguly Thukral (eds). op. cit., pp. 171-184.

Fernandes, Walter. 1991. "Power and Powerlessness: Development Projects and Displacement of Tribals," *Social Action*, 41 (n.3, July-Sept.), pp. 243-270.

Fernandes, Walter. 1994. *Development-Induced Displacement in the Tribal Areas of Eastern India*. New Delhi: Indian Social Institute (mimeo).

Fernandes, Walter, J.C. Das and Sam Rao. 1989. "Displacement and Rehabilitation: An Estimate of Extent and Prospects," in Walter Fernandes and Enakshi Ganguly Thukral (eds). op. cit. pp. 62-88.

Fernandes, Walter and S. Anthony Raj. 1992. *Development, Displacement and Rehabilitation in the Tribal Areas of Orissa*. New Delhi: Indian Social Institute.

Fernandez, Aloysius. P. 1990. "No Dam is an Island," in Aloysius P. Fernandez (ed). *Workshop on Rehabilitation of Persons Displaced by Development Projects*. Bangalore: Institute for Social and Economic Change and MYRADA, pp. 32-43.

Ganguly Thukral, Enakshi. 1989. "Dams: For Whose Development?" in Walter Fernandes and Enakshi Ganguly Thukral (eds). op. cit. pp. 39-61.

Hansda, Subotu. 1983. "Agricultural Development in Tribal Areas," in S. N. Mishra and Bhupinder Singh (eds). *Tribal Area Development*. New Delhi: Society for the Study of Regional Disparities, pp. 21-26.

Kurien, C.T. 1967. *Poverty and Development*. Madras: CLS Publications.

Mahapatra, L.K. 1990. "Rehabilitation of Tribals Affected by Major Dams and Other Projects in Orissa," in Aloysius P. Fernandez (ed). op. cit. pp. 84-98.

Morse, Bradford and Thomas Berger. 1992. *Sardar Sarovar: Report of the Independent Review*. Ottawa: Resources Futures International Inc.

NCA. 1986. *Sardar Sarovar Project Resettlement and Rehabilitation Programme: A Supplementary Report.* Bhopal: Narmada Control Authority.

NIUA. n. d. *Sardar Sarovar. Human Resettlement: A Strategy.* New Delhi: National Institute of Urban Affairs.

Planning Commission. 1956. *The Second Five Year Plan.* New Delhi: Planning Commission, Govt. Of India.

Sharma, B.D. 1978. *Tribal Development: The Concept and the Frame.* New Delhi: Prachi Prakashan.

Sharma, B.D. 1993. "Community Control over Natural REsources and Industry: The Significance of the Mavalibhata Declaration," in Walter Fernandes (ed). *The Indigenous Question: Search for an Identity.* New Delhi: Indian Social Institute, pp. 107-122.

Singh, Chatrapati. 1989. "Rehabilitation and the Right to Property," in Walter Fernandes and Enakshi Ganguly Thukral (eds). op. cit. pp. 91-103.

Singh, Shekar, Ashish Kothari and Kulan Amin. 1992. "Evaluating Major Irrigation Projects in India," in Enakshi Ganguly Thukral (ed). *Big Dams, Displaced People: Rivers of Sorrow, Rivers of Change.* New Delhi: Sage Publications, pp. 169-186.

Vaswani, Kalpana. 1992. "Rehabilitation Laws and Policies: A Critical Look," in Enakshi Ganguly Thukral (ed). op. cit. pp. 155-168.

World Bank. 1994. *Resettlement and Development: The Bankwide Review of Projects Involving Involuntary Resettlement, 1986-1993.* Washington D.C.: Environment Department, The World Bank.

INDEX